Controversy and Complexity

Controversy and Complexity

Canadian Immigration Policy during the 1980s

GERALD E. DIRKS

McGill-Queen's University Press
Montreal & Kingston • London • Buffalo

Legal deposit first quarter 1995
Bibliothèque nationale du Québec

Printed in Canada on acid-free paper

McGill-Queen's University Press is grateful to the
Canada Council for support of its publication program.

Canadian Cataloguing in Publication Data

Dirks, Gerald E., 1942–
    Controversy and complexity: Canadian immigration
    policy during the 1980s
    Includes bibliographical references and index.
    ISBN 0-7735-1238-1
    1. Canada – Emigration and immigration – Government
    policy. I. Title.
    JV7225.D47 1995   325.71   C94-900744-7

Typeset in Palatino 10/12
by Caractéra production graphique, Quebec City

Contents

Preface

In this final decade of the twentieth century, only half a dozen countries have comprehensive immigration policies directed at recruiting, selecting, and resettling people who seek to permanently establish themselves in a state other than the one in which they were born. Instead, the majority of countries today are concerned with problems caused by their own unprecedented population growth, which is frequently exacerbated by intense migration pressures at their frontiers from equally or even more densely populated neighbouring states. While it is not simple to identify all the factors that together make a state appealing to would-be immigrants, there are at least some general social, economic, and political characteristics that appear to be significant. To illustrate, people migrate to join friends and family members who have preceded them, to seek a higher standard of living, and to acquire physical security for themselves and their dependants in a politically stable environment. From the standpoint of prospective immigrants, Canada, for much of its existence, has been high on the list of desirable destinations.

As a country that has received approximately 5 million immigrants and refugees since the end of World War II, Canada has been compelled to expend substantial energy on formulating policies and regulations to cope with the seemingly endless queue of hopeful migrants. A plethora of domestic and external factors have always influenced both the content and direction of Canadian immigration policy. Like other fields of public policy, immigration is strongly affected by interests and questions from both within and beyond government. Some examples include economic concerns related to job opportunities, social considerations related to family reunification, and humanitarian issues arising from the international refugee phenomenon created by human beings' inhumanity to each other.

Moreover, the means adopted to implement and manage immigration programs can constitute a most important ingredient of both what the policy will be and how successfully it can be achieved. The process by which immigrants are selected, the competing priorities of administrative units within or between government departments, and philosophical divergences among influential politicians and bureaucrats all have an impact on what finds its way into policy, and on whether it is effectively yet fairly put into practice.

The objective of the following chapters is to describe and analyse some of the more significant forces and factors that have influenced the formulation and administration of policy. This analysis focuses almost exclusively on the period beginning with the coming into force of Bill C-24, the *Immigration Act* proclaimed in 1978, and ending at the close of 1990. The epilogue, written substantially later than the main body of the book, examines briefly why new immigration legislation was introduced in June 1992 to amend the prevailing Act, and provides an overview of its content and purposes. The 1980s, the era emphasized in this study, were in many ways a microcosm of the overall field of immigration policy in Canadian history. Many of the immigration issues that required attention during this period had exercised earlier generations of Canadians and public policy makers, and continue to do so now in the mid-1990s. However, policy makers during the 1980s also faced unprecedented problems resulting from a more complex domestic and international environment.

The book's eleven chapters and epilogue are grouped into three sections. Part One identifies some of the causes of global migration, discusses how the state system has attempted to deal with flows of humanity, and briefly describes Canada's immigration tradition. Part Two focuses on the major elements or components of Canada's contemporary immigration policy, and explains their overall significance. Among these are how annual immigrant intake targets are set, and what factors impede or facilitate their attainment; the question of eligibility for permanent residence; the costs and benefits of a universal visa policy; the distinction between refugees and immigrants and the differences in the assumptions behind policies related to each; the role of the provinces in this shared policy realm; and the relationship between immigration and demographic issues. Finally, Part Three examines the organizational structure in which immigration policy was formulated and administered during the period covered, as well as some of the managerial approaches adopted and their impact on policy.

A number of hypotheses or premises are enunciated at appropriate points in this study. In virtually every chapter I attempt to demonstrate that economic factors, while undoubtedly major determinants of immigration policy, are not always the most important ones. This volume argues that social and political factors, as well as structural, organizational, and bureaucratic considerations, have had a pivotal impact on both the content of policy and on how it has been implemented.

Most of the research for this study took place between 1987 and the close of 1990, and was largely made possible by the willingness of senior officials at the Canada Employment and Immigration Commission to give me access to immigration policy files. I am most grateful to the then Executive Director of the Immigration Program, J.B. Bissett, and his officials for their substantial assistance, both in directing me to particular file collections and in granting me numerous interviews. I am also indebted to a number of key officials at the Departments of External Affairs and Health and Welfare for so willingly meeting with me to answer my many questions.

I should like to express my gratitude for the support my research received from the Social Sciences and Humanities Research Council, and for the sabbatical, leave of absence, and other vital assistance granted to me by Brock University. These forms of assistance contributed significantly to my ability to spend the required time at the Immigration Program's national headquarters (NHQ).

I should also like to thank Lee Blue and Judy Davies who, for extended periods during 1987 and 1988, assisted me in my research at CEIC headquarters, and Nicole Martin and Andrew Kovacs, who later assisted me in St. Catharines.

The unflagging support Dr. Donald Akenson of McGill-Queen's University Press offered throughout the extended time this volume was in preparation was of immense help to me. Similarly, the fine advice graciously proposed by my copy editor, Avivah Wargon, has served to strengthen this book.

Finally, I want to express my gratitude to my wife for her patience and advice throughout the seemingly endless years this manuscript has been in preparation, and her welcome editorial assistance in the final stages of the work. Full responsibility for any remaining errors belongs to me.

PART ONE

The Immigration Phenomenon

1 Migration: Past and Present

Throughout history, humanity has demonstrated nomadic, restless characteristics. No single factor explains this migratory tendency. Rather, a complex assortment of circumstances and motives contribute to this persistent characteristic of human beings. In general, people have migrated over the ages because of dissatisfaction with prevailing circumstances combined with a somewhat inexplicable sense of optimism that suggests more favourable conditions can be found elsewhere. Stated most simply, human migration takes place because of a variety of push-and-pull forces. While such an explanation is admittedly both incomplete and superficial, it nevertheless identifies the two broad categories of causes and motives.

Before the development and emergence of comparatively safe and rapid modes of transport, population movements were limited to what we would consider today relatively short distances. While prevailing conditions may have been unpleasant in the particular environment in which individuals were living, the thought of a long, dangerous trek that could imperil life and property was usually enough to deter migration over long distances. Until a few centuries ago, migrating with one's dependants and possessions to the next valley or beyond the next range of mountains constituted a major undertaking. Now, while the factors influencing any decision to relocate may be more numerous and complex than in the past, the physical act of travelling – many thousands of kilometres in most circumstances – has become far less stressful and uncomfortable.

When one examines the motives behind human migration more thoroughly, it quickly becomes apparent that the factors prompting the decision to move require more precise categorization and classification than the mere labels of pull and push. Several academic disciplines have, as part of their focus, attempted partial explanations for human migration. Sociology has concentrated on group pressures, both positive and negative, that are seen to promote or inhibit migratory activity. Psychology, for its part, has identified individual emotional or behavioural factors. Economics has contributed explanatory hypotheses based on cost-benefit analysis and the rational choice model. Students of migration have therefore drawn on the research and approaches of a variety of social science disciplines in an effort to comprehend migratory causes and patterns.[1] Academics interested in migration have sometimes developed elaborate models and conceptual frameworks in an effort not only to explain population flows but also to predict where and when they may occur.[2]

Experts agree that no single reason accounts for the decision to migrate. The few examples above indicate some of the approaches that have been adopted to identify these causes. There are, indeed, interconnected reasons that combine to affect the decision. A few of the more obvious include the influence of one's peers, the ability to return to one's homeland should the move prove to be in error, and the intensity of the feeling that a better way of life is possible through migration.

The emergence of the state as the most powerful regulator of societal activity has had a major impact on migratory motives and scope. The increasing pervasiveness of state activity in the daily lives of citizens has both caused and impeded human migration across political frontiers everywhere. Governments routinely, and quite properly in the view of their citizens, establish policies that run the gamut from prohibiting emigration or immigration to promoting them. Whatever the content of a given policy, it can usually be attributed to several factors, including the nature of the political system and culture, economic and commercial interests as perceived by the government, and demographic realities as understood by the authorities. In this century, the volume of people seeking to cross state frontiers has led to the development of complex policies for the selection or exclusion of foreigners. As a corollary, sophisticated administrative machinery to enforce these policies and the accompanying regulations has also been put in place.

State sovereignty then stands at or near the top of the list of factors that presently affect international migration. The doctrine and precepts of sovereignty serve to legitimize government policies that encourage or discourage the admission and departure of people. The question of who can or cannot enter a state has become a highly emotional issue. The international community, for example, has been struggling at least since the 1920s with how to treat bona fide refugees, persons who are in search of sanctuary from infringements on their human rights. Governments are more than a little reluctant to agree to international arrangements that would have the effect, or give the appearance, of eroding what they see as their sovereign right to grant or withhold permission to enter.

Thus examining human migration, particularly across international boundaries, requires recognizing a complex mix of variables. Some originate with the individual, some are environmental, and others have their basis in the prevailing doctrine of state sovereignty.

In the 1980s, First World governments began to discuss the possibility of joint action and cooperative policies to cope with actual or threatened massive population upheavals originating in the Third World. Estimates in the early 1990s suggest that between 70 and 80 million people are actively searching for new homelands. Most of these people reside in the less developed states, where social and economic conditions are perceived to be less attractive than those in the more industrialized, affluent First World. Of this mass of humanity, an estimated 12 to 15 million are legitimate refugees, having been compelled to flee from their countries of origin by persecution or a well-founded fear of it.

Today, First World governments are considering some collaboration on the construction of a series of barriers that will effectively close loopholes and prevent unwanted, undocumented migrants or refugees from gaining admission to their countries. Only people who are properly screened and selected and have appropriate documentation are permitted to enter these states and, even then, the number of countries willing to receive immigrants is dwindling. Operating through such multilateral structures as the Organization for Economic Co-operation and Development and the Council of Europe, like-minded governments, particularly the members of the European Community, have been meeting from time to time since the mid-1980s to share information about policy modifications. These intergovernmental deliberations supplement ongoing discussions within the Office of the United Nations High Commissioner for Refugees and are concerned with the perceived need to more effectively control what authorities refer to as irregular migratory movements. Particular attention is paid to so-called asylum seekers who, while in transit, frequently destroy their valid travel documents and then approach officials at ports of entry claiming refugee status. It is unlikely that the immense population pressures emanating from the less developed states will decrease in the foreseeable future.

The need or compulsion to regulate the population flow, as if it were an inanimate commodity, has become paramount for governments. The regulatory process enables governments, operating in defence of what they perceive to be the public interest, to be selective, welcoming only immigrants who are related to their own citizens, who are believed to possess useful skills, or who have cultural characteristics similar to those of the indigenous population. Nevertheless, desperate and determined people who believe that their present living conditions are intolerable will adopt whatever means are available to undercut controls in their sometimes frantic attempts to attain a more satisfactory life for themselves and their dependants.

The United States, more than any other country, has traditionally been regarded by the world's economically deprived and politically persecuted peoples as the most desirable destination – the pot of gold at the end of the rainbow. During the past forty years American immigration authorities have been confronted by a flood of illegal entrants crossing into their country over its southern boundary. Literally millions of former residents of the Latin American republics have found their way, without screening or processing, into America's large and small cities. This crush of economically and politically motivated – and often desperate – people represents the biggest and most chronic migratory problem confronting the Americans. However, major migratory movements are certainly not unique to that country. The states of Western Europe, along with Australia and Canada, have experienced mounting pressures at their frontiers and ports of entry.

While the impulse to migrate dates from antiquity, at certain times it has been more emphatic and harder to repress. This has been especially true during the past quarter century when improved communications and transportation have made residents of many Third World states painfully aware of the vast disparities between their lifestyles and those of the more affluent societies of the developed countries. Virtually all the countries most popular with would-be immigrants possess comparatively stable economies and liberal-democratic political systems in which individual rights are held to be of the greatest significance. The governments of these states are very critical of other countries that impede or prohibit the movement of their citizens abroad. Yet many of these same liberal-democratic governments have erected barriers to the entry of citizens of authoritarian governments, even if they could acquire exit visas. On the one hand Western countries somewhat hypocritically assert that individuals everywhere have the right to leave their homelands and enjoy freedom of movement, while on the other hand they rigorously contend that they have the sovereign right to select who should be admitted to their countries as visitors or permanent residents. In other words, while Western governments may assert that people have a right to leave a country, they do not acknowledge any such automatic right to enter one. This inconsistency troubles many proponents of human rights.

During the twentieth century, the number of states prepared to welcome immigrants has sharply diminished. Both before and after World War I, the governments of the western hemisphere and those of the old British Dominions encouraged Europeans in search of a new homeland to emigrate. The worldwide depression of the 1930s and World War II drastically curtailed international migration. While the pressures to migrate, both political and economic, abounded in the years after 1945, the number of receiving states with comparatively generous provisions for admitting immigrants shrank to only a few, led by the United States, Canada, and Australia. At the same time, global migratory patterns were shifting. Latin Americans, Asians, and ultimately Africans replaced Europeans as the waves of humanity seeking to migrate grew. By the 1960s Western Europe itself, having recovered from the ravages of war, not only required all of its own population to meet labour market requirements but also recruited guest workers from southern Europe, the Near East, and northern Africa to fill the demand for various types of labourers. Moreover, the breakdown of old European colonial empires and the transformation of their former possessions into independent states resulted in tens of thousands of colonials returning to the Netherlands, Belgium, France, Portugal, and Britain.

Western European governments, unlike those of traditional states of immigration such as Canada and the United States, had little experience with immigrants. Few governments had schemes in place to assist in the adjustment and settlement of newcomers or returning nationals from abroad.[3] With the economic downturn in the early to mid-1970s, Western Europe's need for foreign labour disappeared. Most of the guest workers lost their jobs and were encouraged to return home. Many foreigners, however, desperate to remain in the comparative affluence of Western Europe, have used all available means, legal and illegal, to avoid returning to their homelands.

Migrants seeking out the First World have been motivated by far more than relatively well paying work. The stability here stands in sharp contrast to the wars, civil disorder, oppression, and economic turmoil that have so often prevailed in many parts of the developing world. The unrest and violence in the Near and Middle East, along with wars of self-determination or tribal revenge in north-east and sub-Saharan Africa, as well as those in Southeast Asia, have uprooted hundreds of thousands more. Since the late 1970s, millions more have fled the wars in Afghanistan and Central America.

The litany of factors or motives behind massive population shifts could go on indefinitely. Perhaps in a world accommodating more than five billion people, the fact that seventy to eighty million are uprooted should not be all that amazing. What may be unsettling, however, are the rigorous measures the few remaining traditional states of immigration continue to contemplate or adopt to prevent the entry of people searching for a better way of life. The prohibitions, in the form of rigid regulations, only deepen the plight of millions of would-be and actual migrants. These restrictive immigration policies notwithstanding, migration by self-selected persons persists. Despite the attempts of Western governments to guard their frontiers and ports of entry more zealously, this segment of humanity, with very little to lose, continues to come up with strategies to defeat the gatekeepers.

2 The Emergence of an Immigration Tradition in Canada

Canada's stature in the twentieth century as a prosperous member of the international state system with a developed economy and a skilled labour force is largely attributable to immigration. Regardless of this, many Canadians of every era have expressed doubts about the customs and characteristics of the newcomers in their midst.

Europeans intent on establishing permanent settlements in what became Canada first reached this land at the beginning of the seventeenth century. During the next three centuries, Canada's population grew slowly. Estimates suggest that at the time of the British conquest in 1763 the European population stood at approximately 60 thousand. By Confederation in 1867, the number had reached 3 million, composed primarily of British and French stock. As the twentieth century opened, the 1901 census put the Canadian population at barely 5 million.[1] By midcentury, Canada's population had grown to more than 13 million, and its ethnic composition had shifted markedly from the earlier British and French domination. Until that time, immigration to Canada had been almost exclusively European or American. In the 1950s, 84.6 per cent of immigrants then alive and residing in Canada were European by birth. Canada's immigration policy between Confederation and the mid-twentieth century consistently favoured people from northern and western Europe as well as from the United States. Despite this preference, by 1900 the need to attract farmers to fill the vast Canadian West caused government immigration officials and railroad company land agents to accept applicants from eastern and southern Europe.[2]

A perennial discussion goes on in Canada about the types and numbers of people who should be admitted as immigrants. A substantial and not entirely reconcilable series of factors has shaped the thinking of policy makers. Some of the more long-standing of these include the preferred ethnicity of immigrants, wide-ranging views of the country's absorptive capacity as measured by a variety of criteria, and the economy's presumed labour market requirements over the years. Depending upon the era, prevailing social values, and the health of the economy, differing arguments have been advanced favouring or deploring the admission of immigrants. A consensus within Canadian society has been difficult if not impossible to achieve. As hinted at here but asserted more strenuously in subsequent chapters, this study argues that Canadian governments have consciously avoided encouraging extended public debate on immigration issues because of the divisive nature of the subject.

Until the 1970s, in fact, the Canadian government chose not to explain the objectives of its immigration policy except in the most general terms. Prime Minister Mackenzie King, in May 1947, provided such a general overview in an address to the House of Commons. The contents of his statement became the guidelines that influenced the thinking of politicians and officials for the next two decades. He stated that the fundamental character of the Canadian population mix would not be changed over the subsequent years. The ethnic balance or characteristics of the society, in other words, were set and were not to be altered.[3] Thus Canada would continue to receive people from the traditional source regions, namely, Europe and the United States. Not until the mid-1960s would the country reject this implicitly all-white immigration policy.

Pressure to modify much of the prevailing immigration policy, including its all-white features, was building from several sources within and beyond Canada through the late 1950s and early 1960s. Externally, the world had changed. European empires had dissolved, giving rise to dozens of newly independent states in Asia, Africa, and the Caribbean. Canada endeavoured to establish and maintain good relations with these new governments. Having an immigration policy that in practice excluded nonwhites substantially impeded these efforts.

Within Canada, internationalist interest groups, the churches, organized labour, and many liberal-minded Canadians criticized immigration policy for its racially discriminatory aspects. In an era when South Africa was being condemned for its apartheid policies and Australia was being pointed at for maintaining policies preferential to white immigration, Canadians could not be indifferent to their own government's practices and programs.

Responding to these and similar pressures, the Canadian government, in a series of regulatory modifications beginning in 1962, altered prevailing policy. Major changes occurred in 1967 as the government instituted a new set of criteria for determining the eligibility of applicants for landed immigrant status. Succinctly put, the revised policy awarded specific numbers of points to would-be immigrants on the basis of such criteria as age, education, occupational skills, language capabilities in English and French, and degree of kinship with persons already in Canada. Applicants obtaining a minimum of fifty out of a possible ninety points were eligible to be landed. With these revisions in policy and regulations, the last vestiges of formal racial discrimination disappeared from Canadian immigration policies. People, no matter where they resided in the world, would be processed under the point system. At the same time, an improved process for hearing appeals from rejected applicants or their sponsors in Canada was put in place with the restructuring of the Immigration Appeals Board.[4] Additional immigration posts were opened in Third World areas while extra visa officials were assigned to several heavily used offices. These alterations in policy and regulations soon resulted in noticeable shifts in the regions from which immigrants originated. The traditionally busy offices in London and Rome were surpassed by newly opened or better staffed offices in New Delhi, Hong Kong, and Kingston, Jamaica.

By the mid-1980s, the percentage of immigrants born in Europe had slipped to 28.6. Between 1981 and 1986, 42 per cent of all immigrants entering Canada were born in Asia and almost 64 per cent had Third World origins.[5] The 1981 census indicated that approximately one-third of Canada's population was neither British nor French in origin. Should the immigration intake continue to contain a relatively similar ethnic mix through to the end of this century, the "other" category will constitute the largest segment of Canada's population.

Throughout much of Canada's history, immigration as a segment of public policy has not achieved an especially high profile or a separate or independent departmental home. Rather than being given their own, exclusive organizational base, immigration policy and administration have been combined since Confederation with other government policy responsibilities. Between 1867 and the mid-1890s, immigration was housed in the Department of Agriculture. Since immigrants at that time were selected primarily to open the West, this choice of departments may have been appropriate. From the late nineteenth century until 1919, immigration was housed in the Department of the Interior. In 1919 it moved to the Department of Immigration and Colonization, where it remained through the mid-1930s. Between 1936 and 1949, responsibility for immigration fell to a somewhat unlikely department, that of Mines and Resources. After that, immigration policy formulation and implementation were the responsibility of the Department of Citizenship and Immigration until 1966, and then of the Department of Manpower and Immigration, which subsequently became Employment and Immigration.[6]

Since Confederation, constitutional responsibility for immigration has been divided between the federal and provincial levels of government. In section 95 of the 1867 *British North America Act*, now the *Constitution Act, 1867*, immigration is defined as a concurrent power. In practice, however, for much of Canada's history the federal government dominated this policy area with only occasional objections from provincial authorities. The provinces preferred to have Ottawa accept the political burdens and responsibility associated with immigration rather than become embroiled themselves in an unrelentingly emotional area of public controversy. In the view of most provincial leaders, there were too many dangers and too few rewards connected with almost every aspect of immigration. This assessment began to change in the 1960s when the provinces, especially Quebec but to a lesser degree Ontario too, came to feel that authority in this area could be useful. The role of the provinces in the field of immigration in more recent years is elaborated on in chapter 8.

Economic determinants, more than any other considerations, are usually thought to have shaped the nature and direction of Canadian immigration policy over the past century. In the early post-Confederation years, Canadian immigration programs, unsophisticated to be sure, sought to attract farmers to develop the West and to grow commodities to increase Canadian exports. As the forest and mining industries grew, immigrant labour was perceived as an important factor in helping these components of the economy mature and remain financially competitive in the world export markets. More recently, as the need for unskilled labourers with strong backs was replaced by a new requirement for skilled tradesmen, technicians with high levels of advanced training, and managers, employers endeavoured to persuade immigration officials to recruit this type of applicant.

It was possible at least until the 1960s to estimate the size of immigration movements with surprising accuracy merely by observing the health of the Canadian economy. The unquestioned reliance on labour-market and other purely economic criteria to explain and justify annual immigration flows, however, has lessened since the mid-1960s. This has resulted from the marked rise in the numbers and political significance of refugees, people in refugee-like situations, and people admitted under provisions of family reunification regulations. Without doubt, during Canada's first century economic determinants played the major role in shaping immigration policy. If conditions were prosperous and employment was high, the gates for immigrants were opened wider. When the economy encountered a downturn, the gates were at least partially closed and the flow of immigrants decreased. This most primitive approach to immigration planning – the tap-on and tap-off system – continued in use by immigration authorities well into the 1960s.[7]

Drafting major immigration legislation and guiding it through Parliament has always been a daunting prospect for governments. Protracted debates on immigration issues, whether inside or outside Parliament, have been discouraged by the political party in power: governments have found them to be emotionally charged and potentially corrosive to national unity. Before the passage of the comprehensive act in the late 1970s, there had been only two previous immigration acts in this century, in 1906 and 1952. On most occasions, governments chose a much less politically burdensome approach to making policy, that of the order in council, which modified regulations and procedures. By the early 1970s, however, the extensive changes to immigration policy that seemed necessary could no longer be implemented using the 1952 Act's provisions. Any sweeping alterations would necessitate the passage of a new immigration act.

After several false starts, substantial movement to commence the lengthy process became evident. The responsible minister, Robert Andras, announced in September 1973 that a green paper containing immigration policy options was being prepared and would be completed and released for public discussion within months. For a variety of reasons, including the calling of a general election, the document was not tabled in Parliament until early 1975. The paper, entitled *The Canadian Immigration and Population Study*, represented only the second occasion ever that a Canadian government had presented a comprehensive analysis of immigration policy, and the first time that public input for a new act had actually been solicited. A Special Joint Committee of the Senate and House of Commons toured Canada during 1975 and received oral and written submissions from organizations and individual Canadians with widely diverging views on the direction future immigration policy should take. The committee's report and recommendations ultimately became the basis for the new legislation. Simultaneously with the work of the committee, a legislative drafting group within the Department of Manpower and Immigration, as it was then called, drew up in legal language possible content for any new legislation, which was then circulated among senior officials for comment. Following thorough deliberations not only in the House of Commons, but also in the Standing Committee on Labour, Employment and Immigration, the *Immigration Act*, Bill C-24, was passed during the summer of 1977 and came into force in April 1978.[8]

The *Immigration Act, 1976*, as it is known, constituted the most liberal piece of immigration legislation ever to become law in Canada. The Act showed a positive emphasis and set as immigration priorities the reunification of families, humanitarian and compassionate consideration of refugees, and the promotion of programs satisfying Canada's economic, social, demographic, and cultural goals.[9] The Act formalized policy assumptions and expectations never before enshrined in a statute. Moreover, it expanded or clarified elements of the 1952 Act still believed to be worth maintaining. Canada, for the first time, had immigration legislation that came close to encompassing a consensus of views, in a policy area that had traditionally been divisive and politically dangerous.

More specifically, the *Immigration Act, 1976* established a family class category. Along with sponsorship provisions for relatives, this category ensured that the objective of reuniting families, a cornerstone of immigration policy since World War II, would continue to rank high among government priorities. The creation of a refugee class as one of the categories for applicants encouraged the expectation that Canada would increase its participation in intergovernmental efforts to resettle refugees promptly and compassionately.

At the time of its passage the *Immigration Act, 1976* attracted more support from informed groups and individuals than had any previous legislation in this field. These informed members of Canadian society were optimistic because legislation included features desired by most of the interests traditionally concerned with immigration policy and programs. Ethnic organizations appreciated the high priority given to family reunification, which enabled blood relatives to be brought together. Humanitarian and church groups believed that including provisions to assist refugees in the Act (for the first time) ensured that the interests of those in need would be attended to routinely and not just during international crises as had happened in the past. Employers believed the Act's inclusion of an "independent" class, with accompanying regulations, would help them in their efforts to recruit needed skilled personnel from abroad. (People could be admitted to Canada as members of the independent class if they attained a certain score on a point system, based on such factors as education, job skills, language proficiency, age, and degree of kinship with people already in Canada.) At least at the outset, then, the Act was well received. The legislation endeavoured to combine a host of elements and goals while supporting the expectation that the day-to-day administration of policy would also be effective, combining both facilitation and control measures.

The administration of the 1976 Act, however, has not been without its difficulties. In the years the legislation has been in force, extensive modifications to the regulations have been required. Supplementary legislation was actually needed by the late 1980s and early 1990s to cope with changing domestic and external economic, demographic, and migratory conditions, and the changing concerns of humanitarians. Other impediments to smooth, unencumbered administration of the policy have included attempts to gain landed status from within Canada, extensive efforts by thousands of visitors to acquire employment authorizations (written permission, provided by immigration officials, to work in Canada), and the unexpectedly heavy use of the appeal procedures.

Well over one million people have immigrated to Canada during the life of the 1976 Act. The movement has been composed of members of the family class, refugees and "designated" classes, entrepreneurs, self-employed trades- and craftspeople, retirees, adoptees, and more. They have settled in every region of the country, though most have selected Ontario, Quebec, and British Columbia. In addition, hundreds of thousands of people annually enter Canada as temporary workers, and millions more as visitors, arriving at airports or at the many land entry points along the United States border.

While Canada is seen as a traditional state of immigration, the policies that have been in place during this country's existence have not been particularly popular with society generally. Even under the 1976 Act, which almost achieved consensus among informed organizations at its passage, 42 per cent of those surveyed during 1980 believed too many immigrants were arriving, while only 44 per cent felt that the numbers permitted to enter were appropriate.[10] Seven years later, in a similar poll, only 42 per cent of those polled supported the annual immigration levels.[11]

The remaining parts of this book describe and analyse some of the major characteristics and components of Canadian immigration policy and programs as they have operated under the provisions of the 1976 Act. The analysis focuses in part on the diverse factors that have shaped the content and administration of these programs. Moreover, the roles played by a growing number of institutional and nongovernmental actors in the policy process also receive attention.

Human migration, as these opening chapters have indicated, is a phenomenon as old as mankind. The motives for population movements are varied and complex. With the evolution of the state system and its inherent practices of sovereignty, regulating migration has become a major ingredient in public policy, particularly today in states of the First World. Over time, Canadian governments have adopted a policy stance that they have asserted coincides with national objectives and interests. After examining some of the more significant components of present-day Canadian immigration policy, I analyse the actual processes that gave rise to them. It is these policy components that users today depend on for the effective and fair delivery of programs.

PART TWO

The Philosophy and Content of Canadian Immigration Policy

Describing the precise content of contemporary Canadian immigration policy comprehensively in a volume such as this may be a worthwhile or even ideal objective, but is impossible to achieve in practice. Identifying all the features of any complex, dynamic social policy, which is never static, raises a host of obstacles. Immigration constitutes such a policy area.

Canada's immigration policy and regulations exist in a combined domestic and global environment that is continuously changing. Thus, between the time this manuscript is completed and the time it is readily available to readers, the factors that dictate the specific content of policy and related regulations will, in all likelihood, have altered significantly. Unanticipated social unrest in Canada may have caused policy makers to slow the intake of immigrants. Or, more probably, unexpected political instability in an already overcrowded, less developed country may have produced an enormous exodus of migrants that, in turn, may have resulted in Canada admitting an unusually large number of landed immigrants. Administrative and managerial alterations in day-to-day standard operating procedures, for that matter, may have resulted in a surprising shortfall, or even an increase, in the number of immigrants arriving annually. None of these, or any other variables drawn from a vast range of unpredictable situations, can be accurately taken into account when preparing a comprehensive yet detailed description of policy.

While the seven chapters in this part of the study cannot, therefore, claim to identify and discuss all the specifics of current policy and regulations, they do provide an overview and meet at least two objectives. First, they present the general substance of immigration policy including, among other aspects, a discussion of the admissible classes of immigrants, a description of integrative settlement services offered by government and voluntary organizations, and an examination of federal-provincial relations in the constitutionally shared field of immigration. Second, and arising out of the first objective, these following chapters examine and analyze the assumptions behind particular immigration programs and policy choices. The issues examined include why entry visas are selectively required, how the annual intake levels for immigrants are established, and what considerations complicate the refugee status determination process both for claimants already in Canada and for the government.

Finally, the chapters in part 2 contain glimpses of how structural, organizational, and administrative realities contribute to or detract from effective policy management and the quality of service for those using the programs. These aspects are discussed in more detail in part 3.

The chapters in this part have as their starting point a number of premises or hypotheses. While the following three do not exhaust the list, they are pervasive enough to warrant enunciation here. First, for most of the period examined in this study, economic factors such as labour market considerations did not dominate among the several determinants of the size and overall composition of the annual immigrant intake. Second, the elaborate consultation apparatus established by immigration authorities during the period under analysis, presumably to enable the nongovernmental sector of Canadian society to have input into policy, failed to achieve that end. Rather, at least by the mid-1980s, the ministers responsible for immigration and their bureaucrats tented to use the consultations with the business and voluntary sectors as a forum for disseminating information and legitimizing programs and regulations. Third, a constant tension, which could even be described as a struggle, existed between gatekeepers or controllers on the one hand and facilitators on the other, whether they were elected or career policy makers. These and other premises will be developed in this part of the volume.

3 Identifying Canada's Immigration Programs

The Canadian *Immigration Act, 1976*, proclaimed in force in April 1978, and the supplementary legislation that subsequently modified it, contain a blend or mix of elements that in practice cannot be considered as independent units or watertight compartments. In fact, the immigration program is a complex, comprehensive combination of components, each serving a particular purpose in the overall landscape of policy objectives. This chapter identifies the major admissible classes set out in the 1976 Act and briefly explains their significance in overall policy. The degree to which these categories have been modified over the years since the Act's promulgation will be commented on in subsequent chapters.

Some parts of the immigration program have operated smoothly with no significant public or media notice and no need for amendment during the period under examination here. Other parts, such as refugee status determination for claimants already in Canada, have received much attention from within and beyond government and have been an embarrassment to career officials and cabinet ministers alike.

The foundation of immigration policy lies in those features dealing with admissible classes; that is, persons eligible for permanent residence in Canada. The Act provides for the admission of people in the following identifiable categories: the family class, convention refugees and designated classes, and the independent class.[1] Each admissible class satisfies one or more of the objectives identified in the Act. The family class, for example, meets the goal of bringing together families that want to be reunited, a long-standing corner-stone of Canadian policy. The convention refugee and designated classes category aims to satisfy the Act's humanitarian and compassionate aspirations. The independent class is a somewhat broader category which, according to the Act, contributes to the overall economic well-being of the country.[2] Each of these classes warrants some elaboration.

THE FAMILY CLASS

The highest priority in processing applications under the 1976 Act was given to members of the family class, to Convention refugees and to members of the designated classes. The family class constitutes the largest single category of immigrants entering Canada annually, in some years during the 1980s accounting for almost half the intake. As demonstrated in appendix A, family class arrivals have, without exception, made up a high percentage of Canada's annual intake ever since immigration regained momentum in the postwar years.

The family class consists of what in Western culture is often referred to as the nuclear family: spouses, fiancés and fiancées, unmarried children below a specific age, and parents. Policy makers are routinely urged by ethnic organizations and by individuals with more distant relatives abroad to extend the existing definition of the family class to facilitate the admission of such relatives to Canada. These pressures have arisen because a larger percentage of immigrants now come from areas of the world where the extended family is very much part of the accepted culture. Canada's comparatively narrow definition of the family has its basis in what is commonly believed in Canadian practice to make a single household. Traditionally, if not currently, a family household in Canada comprised a husband and wife along with their unmarried, usually minor, children, and occasionally one or more aged, widowed parents. Those relatives that Canada perceives as likely to establish their own households include the married or unmarried siblings of persons already in Canada, along with aunts, uncles, nieces, nephews, and parents under the age of sixty. In 1991, the minimum age requirement for parents who could be sponsored by children already resident in Canada was removed, thus bringing younger parents within the family class. Under the regulations, relatives too distant to qualify as members of the family class fall into an "assisted relatives" category, which forms part of the independent class. These assisted relatives are subject to admission regulations that take economic selection criteria into account, and measure a number of factors, including occupational demand.

The immigration program permits Canadian citizens and permanent residents who meet certain income requirements to sponsor eligible relatives. (The sponsorship of nonrelatives is discussed in chapter 6.) The sponsor is required to guarantee the financial well-being of the newly arrived immigrant for a period of ten years; the acquisition of citizenship by the sponsored relative does not in itself relieve the sponsor of these obligations. Sponsorship breakdown occurs when a sponsor is no longer able or willing to meet the financial commitment. Should this happen, the province in which the sponsored relative resides can seek redress through the courts. This, however, has not proved a particularly serious problem when compared with other difficulties encountered by officials trying to administer immigration programs.

In virtually every admissions component of Canada's immigration programs, overseas and inland officials have the power to exercise discretion. The content of regulations, especially those relating to the family and refugee classes, can arouse profound emotions in sponsors and frequently result in criticism of how this discretionary power is used. Critics point out that officials are not dealing with inanimate commodities but rather with feeling individuals, each possessing different levels of competence and adaptability. An example may illustrate why immigration program managers nevertheless maintain that there is often a good reason – frequently benefiting the applicant or sponsor – for front-line officials to wield discretionary powers.

From time to time, a sponsor wants to bring to Canada a dependant who falls outside the normal eligibility requirements. The person in question may be a son or daughter who at one time has been married, which would normally make that individual inadmissible under family class provisions. However, this would not be the case if, for some reason, the individual manifested the characteristics of a dependant. Immigration headquarters set down guidelines for these and similar situations early in the life of the present Act. "In the main, we feel that where genuine dependency continues, irrespective of age, we should facilitate the admission of the individual concerned through discretion or through an Order-in-Council."[3] Here, as in other instances where guidelines are issued, specific illustrations are not given in discretionary areas because officials could interpret them as being restrictive.[4]

The administration of the family class provisions, including fulfilling the processing requirements, has proven to be time consuming and thus frustrating for sponsors and applicants. Several factors contribute to the lengthy processing time required before visas can be issued. These include verifying the existence of a bona fide relationship between the sponsor and the applicant, obtaining the appropriate medical screening for the would-be immigrant, assessing the sponsor's financial capability to fulfil the guarantee of support, and, for some would-be immigrants, overcoming obstacles to acquire exit visas. Immigration officials also point out that many people, once they receive visas to enter Canada, still take several months to tidy up their personal affairs before emigrating from their homeland.

While the causes of the delay may be numerous, and attributable to individual idiosyncrasies as well as to the formalities of the process, informed observers tend to lay most of the blame at the door of the immigration authorities. Critics, along with some senior officials at Canada Employment and Immigration (CEIC) headquarters, have maintained that the number of immigration visa officials may at times be inadequate to deal promptly with family class applications. The underlying cause for delay, however, continues to be the concern at all levels of the immigration bureaucracy to prevent fraudulent use of the system by applicants or their sponsors. Indeed, some of these fears are justified. As an example, officials do sometimes discover that kinship claims are not valid.

Canadian authorities have become sensitive to the criticisms regarding the time needed to complete processing requirements. Studies within CEIC indicated, for instance, that in 1979 the average time between the initiation of processing and the issuance of a visa stood at 109 days. Just one year later, the average time required had risen to 210 days; by the mid-1980s, it stood at 237 days.[5] The extended time has left large numbers of applicants in the processing pipeline and has skewed the statistics for the actual number of persons reaching Canada during any one year.

One provision associated with the family class, in force until 1990, involved a scheme whereby "the last remaining family members" were permitted to gain admission to Canada even though they might have been, in the strict sense, outside the conventional nuclear family. The objective was to enable an individual, regardless of age, to join the family already in Canada if no other relatives remained in their country of origin. Some kind of dependent relationship, financial or emotional, needed to exist between the individual and the remainder of the family.[6] In an attempt to assure fair and consistent consideration of such applications from sponsors in Canada, guidelines were prepared for immigration officials both at inland centres and overseas. These focused upon the nature and extent of the dependency rather than upon nearness of kinship.[7] This "last remaining family member" scheme was held up by authorities as an example of the compassionate and humanitarian character of immigration policy. The number of people accepted under these rather restrictive provisions, however, did not exceed a few hundred cases annually during the years the scheme was in use.

For a time, potential immigrants did turn to this "last remaining family member" program in an attempt to enter Canada when they were ineligible for admission in any other category. Deteriorating labour market conditions during the early to mid-1980s had resulted in tighter controls on such categories as assisted relatives. Writing in 1984, the then minister of Employment and Immigration, John Roberts, stated: "The question that has taken some time to resolve is precisely how to define the spirit and intent of our humanitarian principles so that all deserving applicants are allowed forward while, at the same time, ensuring the integrity of the special measures which are not intended to be used as a general alternative to normal selection criteria."[8] Once again, the ever present anxiety concerning the possible misuse of programs and the unending zeal for controls were apparent.

Of the three major admissible classes, the family class accounts for the largest portion of the annual arrivals, and requires a sizeable processing staff within and beyond Canada. Except during well-publicized international refugee crises, interest groups pay more attention to family class admissions than to those of any other admissible class. Active lobbyists have over the years acquired skill and sophistication in their efforts to bring more of their kin to this country. At the same time, the family class is the most emotion laden and politically sensitive of all the categories of possible immigrants. Canadian governments, both Liberal and Progressive Conservative, have recognized the political dynamite associated with family reunification. Any suggestion of increasing the independent immigrant class at the cost of reducing the volume of the family class would be a politically inept move on the part of any government.

In order to acquire more immigrants in the independent class without reducing the intake of family class members, the Canadian government announced in the autumn of 1990 a five-year plan that would increase the total annual immigration arrivals. The actual proportion of the annual intake earmarked for members of the family class would remain relatively constant or drop just slightly. The family thus remains a major component of Canadian immigration programs.

CONVENTION REFUGEES AND DESIGNATED CLASSES

Convention refugees and other "designated classes," according to the 1976 *Immigration Act*, have as high a priority as the family class. Unlike family reunification, which has enjoyed preference in immigration policy since World War II, refugees had no statutory recognition prior to the promulgation of this Act. Previously, refugees and other people in refugee-like situations were admitted to Canada, if at all, primarily through the use of ad hoc provisions legitimized by the cabinet. The 1976 Act provided for an admissible refugee class "to fulfil Canada's international legal obligations concerning refugees and to uphold its humanitarian tradition with respect to the displaced and persecuted."[9] As a signatory to the Convention Relating to the Status of Refugees, an instrument Canada had only adhered to in 1969, this country was expected to treat bona fide refugees in accordance with the provisions of that intergovernmental agreement. Refugees were entitled to receive sanctuary and not to be subject to *refoulement* – the act of sending people in danger back to the state which has threatened persecution or worse.

Along with the refugee admission provisions, the Act empowered authorities to establish specific "designated classes" permitting the entry of people in refugee-like situations who did not qualify for assistance under the rigid, legalistic definition in the Refugee Convention. These designated classes are intended once again to demonstrate the humanitarian and compassionate character of Canada's immigration policy. The designated classes established and recognized during the 1980s included one for the Indo-Chinese, another for self-exiles, intended for persons from Eastern Europe, and a third for political prisoners and the oppressed, intended for individuals who had been put in detention by their governments. The designated classes category, supplemented at times by other special humanitarian measures, enables people from countries experiencing political and social domestic turmoil, such as Lebanon and Sri Lanka during the past decade, to enter and remain in Canada at least temporarily, until conditions at home stabilize.

Under the Act and regulations, community based and national voluntary organizations are encouraged to sponsor Convention refugees and members of designated classes. Such organizations negotiate arrangements with federal authorities to assist in the settlement and adjustment of the newcomers to Canadian society. In the late 1970s and 1980s thousands of Indochinese, along with smaller numbers from Central America, benefited from these provisions.

Refugees can obtain permission to enter and remain in Canada through two approaches. The frist, the one expected by the Act's drafters to be the normal entry route, has bona fide refugees being selected by overseas Canadian visa officials from pools of individuals already in states of first asylum. The objective here is to alleviate some of the burden on these asylum states, which are frequently among the less developed countries and already overcrowded. The second approach, the one that during the early and mid-1980s became susceptible to misuse, has persons already in Canada, or arriving at ports of entry, making a claim for refugee status that must then be verified by an involved procedure.

When a refugee takes the first approach, the overseas visa officials measure that person's admissibility using four criteria. First, the applicant must meet the definition of a refugee contained in the Refugee Convention; second, the applicant must not have already acquired permanent residence; third, the applicant must not be part of an inadmissible class as set forth in the Act; and fourth, the applicant, in the view of the processing officer, must be capable of successful establishment in Canada.[10] The importance of the fourth of these criteria was re-emphasized in October 1990, in the *Annual Report to Parliament on Future Immigration Levels*, which asserted that refugees selected abroad are assessed for "their potential for eventual self-sufficiency in Canada."[11] Refugees and members of designated classes selected abroad are entitled to interest-free transportation loans, language training, counselling, and financial assistance.

The overseas selection channel has, for the most part, operated relatively smoothly during the life of the legislation. Some critics from nongovernmental organizations have, however, occasionally commented adversely on a feature or two found in the four criteria for admissibility, especially the one requiring a refugee to be capable of successfully establishing him- or herself in Canada. Put succinctly, the criticism comes from the view that refugees who have fled their homeland for fear of persecution or worse are in need of sanctuary and should not be made to meet admission criteria more appropriate for economic migrants. Informed observers have also questioned why rejected refugee claimants outside Canada are not entitled to some sort of an appeal in the same way that many unsuccessful refugee claimants are in Canada. These and similar observations did not cause nearly the political uproar that occurred when attention shifted to the second channel for refugee admission to Canada.

This second channel, which permits individuals to claim refugee status on their arrival at Canadian ports of entry or, subsequently, at inland immigration centres, has been fraught with problems and ultimately taxed officials' innovative capacities to the hilt. Under earlier immigration legislation, such provisions did not exist. The 1976 *Immigration Act*, however, established an elaborate procedure for verifying claims for refugee status, including provisions for two levels of appeal for rejected claimants, first to the Immigration Appeals Board and finally to the Federal Court. The reason for the establishment of this unprecedented, generous mechanism can be traced to the philosophical outlook of the responsible minister and those senior officials in a position to influence the content of the legislation when it was being drafted during the mid-1970s. These policy makers, including Robert Andras, Minister of Manpower and Immigration, Allan Gotlieb, Deputy Minister, and John Hucker, Chairman of the Legislation Drafting Group in that era, wished to eradicate the rigid and uncompassionate features of former immigration programs.[12] This is not to suggest that no notes of caution regarding such liberalized provisions were sounded by those involved with formulating the new legislation. Writing five months before the law was promulgated, one official perceptively observed,

The new refugee legislation could even more easily be destroyed by a mass influx of economic migrants seeking to obtain a foothold in this country by claiming refugee status at their port of entry. Even more worrying to me is the situation which would occur as a result of a massive and unorganized movement of true refugees. If true refugees arrive at our border, we have no choice but to take them in, but if the number is large and neither controlled or selected, public controversy and general hostility towards the present policy will quickly result.[13]

The procedure for verifying claims for refugee status within Canada encountered problems almost as soon as it came into operation. The most severe and chronic of these arose because of the volume of individuals trying to use this channel for admission, although knowledgeable representatives of immigrant and refugee settlement organizations identified procedural shortcomings as well. The refugee status determination process could only handle a few hundred claimants annually. Before the procedures had even been in force for two years, a backlog of claimants had become apparent. Despite a certain amount of tinkering intended to expedite the process, the numbers in the queue increased. By 1986, the backlog exceeded 18,000 claimants; by the close of 1987, this figure had more than doubled. One of the many in-house committees or task forces struck to study this backlog put its finger on the nub of the problem. "It is evident that the very existence of such a universal mechanism can act as a magnet for persons seeking admission to Canada. This leads to exponential increases in the caseload faced by the status determining body and ultimately results in the collapse of the system and even pressure for a general amnesty."[14]

During the 1980s, immigration officials as well as outside experts devoted dozens of "person years" to developing acceptable alternatives to this hopelessly inadequate procedure for verifying refugee status claims. No other segment of the immigration program required so much attention. The juggernaut proved to be so intractable that, finally, new legislation had to be enacted. As a later chapter indicates, this refugee status determination issue remains politically sensitive and administratively difficult. In part because of their high profile, the significance of refugee issues will persist.

THE INDEPENDENT CLASS

The third admissible category under the provisions of the 1976 *Immigration Act* is the independent class. Virtually everyone who qualifies for admission to Canada as a member of this class is considered to have a direct impact upon the national economy because of his or her probable participation in Canada's labour force. Would-be immigrants in this class, except for entrepreneurial and investor applicants, are assessed under the "point system," by which they earn units based upon factors such as age, education, language, work skills, and their degree of kinship, if any, with people already residing in Canada. As discussed earlier, individuals who have relatives in Canada, but relatives too distant to qualify them for the family class, are labelled "assisted relatives." They form part of the independent class, constituting as much as 25 per cent of that class during some years in the 1980s. Independents constituted between 20 and 30 per cent of the annual immigrant movement during the 1980s, but this proportion is expected to gradually increase. The rationale or justification for the "independent class" appears in section 3(*h*) of the Act, which declares that such people assist in meeting the goal of "fostering and developing a strong viable economy and the prosperity of all regions of Canada."

During the 1980s, the government placed additional emphasis on one segment of the independent class, that designed to bring entrepreneurs and investors to Canada. According to a senior official, "The objective of the business immigration program is to promote, encourage and facilitate the immigration of experienced business persons from abroad who will make a positive contribution to the country's economic development by applying their risk capital and know-how to Canadian business ventures which create jobs for Canadians."[15] Federal officials have worked closely with the provinces in an effort to ensure that the business immigrants who are permitted to enter Canada do, in fact, possess the desired abilities, which are intended to strengthen the economic outlook in specific regions of the country. Since the provinces work directly with industry and small business, they are in an especially good position to advise on whether a proposal submitted by a prospective entrepreneurial immigrant will aid or possibly undermine businesses already in existence.

The independent category is not, however, confined to the capitalist and managerial classes. Other persons admitted under this category include the self-employed, selected workers for occupations with vacancies, and, through 1990, self-supporting retirees and their dependants. The retiree program was discontinued because it was no longer being used as anticipated. The program had been intended for retired people who had been born in Canada. It was terminated when it began to be used mainly by people who had once immigrated to Canada, then left, and, after retiring, wanted to enter a second time. By 1989, only 4 per cent of those entering Canada under this program had been born in Canada.[16]

The independent class has not brought with it nearly the same number of administrative and political difficulties as did the family and refugee classes. A number of factors contribute to the comparative ease with which this portion of the immigration program has been administered. First, as pointed out above, the absolute numbers in this class have, at least until the 1990s, fallen far short of those in the family class. Second, people in the independent class tend not to have the strong advocates in Canada that would-be immigrants in the other admissible classes do: this class lacks the domestic political base useful in acquiring public support. Finally, actual or suspected abuse of policy appears to have been less frequent with this class.

While everyone seeking permanent residence in Canada must qualify in one of the three admissible classes described in this chapter, they are not the only individuals permitted to enter the country. Other regulations and policy provisions deal with foreigners wishing to enter for short terms and specific purposes. Such applicants include students and their spouses, visitors, temporary workers on term contracts, and domestics. People in these categories who are coming here to work require visas and employment authorizations. Officials try to monitor the activities of visaed individuals to ensure they abide by the provisions that legitimize their comparatively short term residences in Canada. Infractions can lead to detention and removal.

Canadian immigration policy, then, authorizes three broad classes of people to enter as permanent residents and admits others for shorter periods of time under specially drafted regulations. Immigration officials aim to administer the entry of all classes expeditiously, without surrendering their equally important responsibility to ensure that policy and regulations are adhered to and that the intake of people is effectively managed and controlled. Policy is administered by personnel from both CEIC and the Department of External Affairs, from offices and ports of entry within Canada and from visa posts abroad. It is formulated and later implemented in an environment affected by a plethora of forces and factors. These range from the pressures mounted by interest groups to the bureaucratic politics and interdepartmental rivalry that are a part of any large organization, be it governmental or private. Moreover, the emotional volatility of immigration issues is never far below the surface.

4 The Annual Immigration Levels Exercise

An earlier chapter referred to the linkages among the elements that make up Canada's immigration policy. While isolating and then focusing on specific parts of the immigration process seems necessary for the sake of explanation and analysis, this approach may not provide an entirely accurate or comprehensive picture of how policy making and administration work in practice. The challenge of setting and then attaining annual immigrant intake levels in Canada does, however, serve as a useful example of how many issues and factors, both independently and collectively, enhance or hinder the Immigration Program's ability to accomplish its task. A host of variables, including pressures for family reunification, provincial preferences and priorities, the state of the economy, and competing interdepartmental objectives, affect how the annual number of immigrants that officials anticipate to be in the public interest is arrived at. The officials responsible for projecting the annual intake are painfully aware of the divergent agendas and complex organizational realities that have to be taken into account before the annual level setting can be successfully completed. This chapter identifies some of the variables that affect the setting and attainment of the annual target level or range: it is not my objective to evaluate the strengths and weaknesses of the economic, social, demographic, or humanitarian arguments put forward by competing agenda-setting bodies.

Two propositions are advanced in this chapter. First, while national and regional economic factors are undoubtedly considered when annual immigration levels are established, other issues and forces have proved to be equally if not more significant in determining the number of people who actually reach Canada in search of permanent residence in any given year. Second, the elaborate consultative processes developed and maintained by immigration officials during the period under analysis have not enabled either the voluntary or business sectors to have much impact on the actual size and composition of the annual immigration intake. Rather, consultations have provided the responsible minister and immigration officials with an opportunity to explain policy and regulations and to brief invited individuals and organizations on forthcoming plans and programs.

Section 7 of the 1976 *Immigration Act* requires the responsible minister to inform Parliament each autumn of the number of immigrants Canada anticipates during the subsequent calendar year: "The minister, after consultation with the provinces concerning regional demographic needs and labour market considerations, and after discussions with such other persons, organizations and institutions as he deems appropriate, shall lay before Parliament ... a report specifying the number of immigrants that the Government of Canada deems it appropriate to admit during any specified period of time, and the manner in which demographic considerations have been taken into account in determining that number."[1] Frequently, the annual projections are supported by background papers, which expand on the reasons for the suggested figures and give a glimpse into the priorities of officials in the Immigration Program (the name given during the 1980s to the branch at CEIC responsible for the formulation and administration of policy within Canada).

When planning the annual immigration intake, officials routinely consider social, economic, and demographic factors. The long-standing objective of family reunification and the needs of Canada's labour market, along with the size, rate of growth, structure, and distribution of population, all shape the annual plan. The fact that family reunification remains the Immigration Program's highest priority attests to its importance as a policy determinant and a constant among the factors that affect the annual immigrant intake projections. The ever present issues of job availability and job creation, combined with the mounting desire of the provinces to attract foreign entrepreneurs and investors, ensure that economic considerations also play a large part in shaping the annual plan. Demography too has been taken into consideration since the 1970s, when policy makers realized that Canada's birth rate had fallen below replacement levels. (They also recognized, of course, that unlimited immigration intake would result in population growth exceeding Canada's absorptive capacity in terms of public funds for housing, social and educational services, and the protection of the environment.)

When identifying the factors affecting the size and composition of the annual immigration flow, conventional wisdom has always placed economic and labour market considerations at the top of the list. This thinking was valid for much of Canada's history, but since the early 1980s economic considerations, while undeniably still important in the minds of immigration policy makers, have no longer been as dominant. A number of reasons account for this change, of which three are highlighted here. First, as the previous chapter points out, certain constants quite apart from economic concerns occupy unchallenged positions in the annual forecasts. Among these are the cornerstone of family reunification, as well as the humanitarian and compassionate interests reflected in the annual provisions for refugees. In some years during the 1980s, family class arrivals constituted 40 per cent or more of all immigration, although they are expected to diminish in the 1990s to between 30 and 35 per cent. Refugees and members of designated classes too have made up as much as 20 per cent of annual arrivals. Second, the number of people applying for landed immigrant status from within Canada rose constantly during the 1980s, until by 1990 it constituted 20 per cent of the annual intake.[2] Many of these applicants were dependants such as children and spouses, and thus gained entry for reasons apart from any economic or labour market considerations. Third, political and organizational forces have had a significant impact on the number and type of immigrants entering Canada each year. For example, from the political standpoint, if it is known that the responsible minister, or for that matter the prime minister, favours increased immigration, this can act as a signal to the officials developing the annual intake plan. At the same time, from the organizational standpoint, annual forecasts must take into consideration how overseas or inland officials are deployed, since this can affect the type and number of immigrants authorized to enter Canada.

The objectives behind the annual immigration plan have often been misunderstood by members of Parliament, interest groups, and the voluntary and business sectors generally. As envisaged by the formulators of the present policy in the mid-1970s, the annual process of determining the appropriate number of immigrants for the subsequent year was not intended to establish a quota or ceiling. Rather, the aim was to give a numerical range or goal that Immigration Program officials believed to be attainable and in Canada's interest. As the years have passed, however, this emphasis on a target range has gradually given way to a sense that, in practice, the figure is more of an upper limit on immigration. In his 1990 annual report, the auditor-general drew attention to the widespread puzzlement about the purposes behind the intake range and urged immigration authorities to justify more explicitly their reasons for announcing a particular figure or range each year.[3]

The annual immigration level is composed of separate figures for each of the admissible classes discussed earlier. Planners develop projections for the family, refugee, and independent classes and combine them into the total yearly target. When planning for the 1976 *Immigration Act* was in its early stages, the drafters thought it would be too difficult to include an accurate refugee class plan in the levels exercise. Refugee situations, they argued, were rather unpredictable and not at all amenable to projections and annual plans. However, the officials involved in preparing the forecasts have always included an annual refugee target, though they have sometimes modified it as circumstances dictated.

The Act instructs immigration planners to consult not only with the provinces, but also with groups and agencies from the voluntary and private sectors that have an interest in the composition of the immigrant flow to Canada. This consultation process has come to include the provinces, nongovernmental organizations from the voluntary sector, other federal departments and agencies affected by immigration, the business community, and, since the early 1980s, the small group of academics who carry out research in this public policy area. Meeting with organizations outside of government recognizes the interest many groups have in immigration issues, including employers, ethnic associations, and agencies providing settlement services to newly arrived immigrants and refugees.[4]

With growing experience, officials at CEIC have developed an array of predictive tools, including statistical simulative models that assist them in formulating realistic and accurate forecasts. Moreover, for at least part of the 1980s they considered demographic factors such as the numbers needed now and in the future to replace the existing population, and their impact on Canadian society. Most of the data for this analysis come from Statistics Canada and from within CEIC; they are supplemented by scholarly research carried out independently or on contract by the academic community. By the 1990s some officials felt that demographic considerations would play a diminished role among the factors being weighed when setting annual target ranges. This change could conceivably be due to the contents of the three-year demographic review undertaken in 1986 by Health and Welfare Canada, which said comparatively little about the connection between immigration and demography.[5]

The planning process, while more systematic and scientific today than at its outset, must also pay attention to issues laden with political ramifications. To illustrate, when estimating the number of selected workers employers seek to bring in, officials must consider whether or not there are job-ready Canadians for the positions these foreign workers are expected to fill.

When first setting annual immigration levels in the late 1970s, senior officials believed that society's attitudes to the size of the immigration flow, as determined through public opinion surveys, should be given some weight. This message was apparent in a memorandum prepared prior to the tabling of the first report to Parliament on immigration levels in 1978. "Social considerations should be evaluated before finalizing immigration levels. Periodic public opinion surveys commissioned by CEIC will help to feel the public's pulse on immigration matters."[6] While such surveys were conducted periodically through the 1980s, their findings failed to have much impact on forecasts. A sense persisted among interest groups and informed members of Parliament, at least in the early years of the annual levels exercise, that, in the preparation of immigration targets, labour market considerations took precedence over other factors, including public opinion.[7] As the 1980s progressed and Canada came out of the depths of an economic recession, the intense concern about labour market conditions was, at least for a time, replaced by a growing awareness in the minds of senior policy makers and their subordinates of social, humanitarian, demographic, and bureaucratic factors.

The statutory requirement to establish an annual immigration range for the subsequent year has encouraged officials to search for and use more data in an effort to enhance their analytical capability and planning. In some instances, raw, unorganized data on recruitment and selection were available to officials but had not been systematically arranged in a form helpful for arriving at projections. The methodologies for setting intake targets have matured over the past decade. The annual exercise, however, continues to depend partly on intuition rather than entirely on scientific rigor. Nevertheless, officials persist in their attempts to improve the quality of their projections.

During the mid-1980s, the unit at the Canada Employment and Immigration Commission's national headquarters (NHQ) that bore the main responsibility for preparing the annual presentation came to devote most of its efforts to this one task. Some senior managers at NHQ believed that the unit in fact spent too much time on this one endeavour, and managed to decrease the time allocated to it.[8] This unit, formerly known as the Migration and Demographic Directorate but in 1988 renamed the Immigrant Policy Unit, solicits and assesses input into the level setting process from immigration centres across the country and from visa posts abroad. Other federal departments and agencies are also invited to provide input and to comment on a draft of the annual report to Parliament, before it goes to cabinet and then is tabled in the House. Among the departments that do express interest are Health and Welfare Canada, responsible for evaluating applicants' medical data, and CSIS (the Canadian Security and Intelligence Service), answerable for security screening of potential immigrants. The impact the proposed number of immigrants will have on personnel resources is probably the chief motivation for these and other government bodies to take an interest.

The completed report to Parliament is normally presented to cabinet in early autumn. In some years, cabinet has sent the report back to Immigration Program officials because the projected targets have not met with approval. Occasionally, officials have prepared an earlier submission to cabinet, usually in the spring. When the spring submission was developed during the early and mid-1980s, it contained answers to questions raised previously by ministers, confidential background papers that might be made public later, and other data the minister responsible for immigration and his advisers believed cabinet should be aware of.

THE RELATIONSHIP BETWEEN CEIC AND DEA

As stated at the beginning of this chapter, the exercise of setting the annual immigration range provides a useful illustration of the linkages between factors influencing immigration policy. Without exaggeration, virtually every aspect of CEIC's relationship with other federal departments, provincial governments, and voluntary organizations affects not only the manner in which the annual estimate is arrived at, but also the likelihood of it being achieved. The lengthy list of those factors would include intangibles such as the willingness of relevant departments to coordinate their activities respecting immigration issues, and concrete matters such as whether these same departments have adequate fiscal and human resources to fulfil their obligations to the immigration programs. The issue of interdepartmental cooperation, particularly between CEIC and the Department of External Affairs (DEA), especially during the early to mid-1980s, warrants separate analysis and is examined later in this study. This discussion is confined to indicating how squabbles over utilizing human resources have had an impact on establishing and meeting the annual target figures.

In the first half of the 1980s immigration officials at CEIC frequently worried about not achieving the annual targeted range. The anxiety stemmed from at least two factors. First, the availability of immigration personnel had a direct impact on the size of the actual annual immigration flow. Second, between 1981 and 1992 responsibility for the formulation of immigration policy rested with the Immigration Program at CEIC, while the delivery and administration of the overseas recruitment and selection programs was done by DEA through its foreign posts.[9] Put simply, if DEA failed to receive adequate funding from the Treasury Board to provide enough officers for the essential overseas processing of applicants, or if the department's senior managers chose to deploy human resources for other tasks, it might not achieve the annual target range set by CEIC. Both immigration officials at CEIC and the responsible minister stood to be embarrassed. Options available to CEIC to reduce this risk included appealing to Treasury Board for additional resources, opening negotiations with DEA aimed at redeploying scarce resources, or publicly acknowledging that government restraint made it necessary to lower the intake figure.

To ensure that the immigrant intake goal would be met, CEIC tried to improve the efficiency and productivity of those administering the programs, both at its own immigration centres within Canada and – through discussions with DEA – at posts abroad. Meetings between representatives of the two federal departments frequently proved difficult and did not always conclude to CEIC's satisfaction. Immigration Program officials felt that overseas posts sometimes used the resources allocated to them for purposes other than processing immigrant applications. DEA, for its part, contended that CEIC was sometimes unrealistic about the number of applicants who could be interviewed, screened, and issued with admission documentation. DEA explained that non-immigrant applicants such as visitors and students, who also required time to process, had actually increased in number at many posts, leaving fewer staff free to deal with family and independent class applicants. These and other contentious issues proved difficult to resolve.[10]

Ministers responsible for immigration and their officials were justifiably concerned about criticism from informed segments of the voluntary and private sector regarding any shortfalls in landing immigrants and refugees (i.e., in the numbers granted landed immigrant status). During the first half of the 1980s when the annual goals were not reached (as shown in appendix C), nongovernmental organizations, joined by opposition MPS, expressed strong dissatisfaction with the efforts of immigration officials. On such occasions the government and its officials, always sensitive to the emotional and political volatility of immigration issues, consciously steered away from any protracted debate on the matter, preferring instead to indicate that the problems, if indeed there were problems, would be addressed promptly.

With the exception of CEIC, the results of the annual exercise of setting immigration targets have usually been taken more seriously beyond government departments than within them. The annual immigration levels document is widely circulated, reaching not only MPS but also hundreds of informed individuals and interest groups quite prepared to be assertive about immigration and refugee issues. Their interests are diverse: for instance, even if the targets set for the admission of family or independent class members are met, those concerned with humanitarian issues will protest loudly if the refugee intake falls short.

During the early 1980s CEIC officials believed that a sizeable backlog of family and independent class applicants awaited processing at several overseas posts, and asked why the annual targets for processing and landing immigrants still failed to be met. In response, External Affairs stated that many applications had been withdrawn and no accumulation of files existed. When the target ranges began to be achieved or surpassed in 1987, the backlog issue disappeared from CEIC's list of irritants, despite the fact that many places, particularly visa offices at Hong Kong, Bangkok, and Manila, did have backlogs. By the 1990s, at these busy East Asian offices, increased migratory pressure had resulted in backlogs of applicant files so extensive that they remained uncounted and well beyond the capacity of officials to process.

The elapsed time between the receipt of an application, the issuance of an entry visa and the applicant's arrival at a Canadian port of entry constituted yet another obstacle to achieving the annual targets. Individuals whose processing began during one calendar year usually did not reach Canada until the following year, thus skewing the intake figures. During 1986, for example, the average time for the completion of processing stood at 227 days. In 1987 this fell to 201 days, but it jumped to 259 days in 1989. What is more, there were large variations in the elapsed times from mission to mission.[11] Additional weeks and months often passed before the visaed applicant finished settling personal affairs in the homeland and arrived in Canada.

On occasion, CEIC has to alter regulations to resolve some administrative anomaly or to deal with a previously unexpected shortfall or surplus of people in a particular occupation. These modifications might take place after the tabling in Parliament of the next year's immigration level targets, and could affect whether or not the annual goals set for immigrant arrivals are met. Regardless of whether the change in regulations is intended to increase or decrease the flow of newcomers, it can take five to six months before the effect becomes noticeable.[12]

While the number of factors that could affect the size of the annual immigrant intake seems endless, during the 1980s DEA also pointed out that the targeted annual range was possibly too narrow. A broader range would increase the probability of achieving the projections and reduce the chances for embarrassment for both CEIC and DEA. Rather than a range of 110,000 to 120,000, for example, External Affairs suggested that unpredictable and uncontrollable circumstances could quite easily justify a broader range, such as 110,000 to 130,000 arrivals.[13] CEIC, however, has continued to set a narrower range, believing the broader one would make the annual exercise less helpful to organizations that use the figures to develop their own immigrant adjustment programs and budgets.

For a time during the mid-1980s, matching the available human resources funded by the Treasury Board to the annual intake level proved to be an even more difficult task than it had been previously. In June 1985 Flora MacDonald, the minister of employment and immigration, announced to Parliament that after much study and consultation the government favoured a "moderate and controlled" increase in immigration.[14] Yet at almost the same time the then deputy prime minister, Eric Nielsen, tabled a report urging significant reductions in government spending on almost all federal activities. To deal with these two conflicting policy pronouncements, several middle- and senior-level immigration officials at headquarters suggested that it would be possible to increase arrivals, even with diminishing personnel, by eliminating some of the more labour-intensive enforcement and control measures still required.[15] Possibly the massive amount of paperwork required of front-line officials could also be reduced. Applications from people wishing to sponsor relatives or refugees could be mailed in and perhaps fewer applicants could be personally interviewed. Moreover, staff at local Canada Immigration Centres might be given more authority when dealing with potential sponsors.[16]

As another result of the government's announced intention to strive for moderate increases in immigration while promoting budgetary restraint, officials looked at whether people already in Canada, such as visitors or students, might be processed here and permitted to remain as permanent residents rather than having to return to their homelands to complete the necessary paperwork. If such a decision had been implemented, it would have lessened the workload of visa officials abroad while increasing that of officials at Canadian immigration offices; however, it was not. The issue of how best to deploy and utilize insufficient human resources remained one of the major debates between the immigration officials at CEIC and DEA, and undoubtedly had substantial impact on whether or not they ultimately achieved the annual target levels. Despite the establishment of interdepartmental committees, progress towards streamlining was slow. Officials at DEA responsible for supervising staff who processed and screened immigrants still felt that their colleagues at CEIC did not always recognize the amount of time needed to train and familiarize staff at overseas posts with policy and regulations. The inevitable time lag, according to these supervisors, could be well over a year.

By the late 1980s annual shortfalls in immigration intakes had given way to arrivals substantially exceeding the proposed annual ranges. This somewhat surprising turn of events resulted from a combination of factors: Treasury Board did gradually increase allocations for personnel following the 1985 announcement calling for moderate but controlled growth; the productivity of visa officers at overseas posts improved; and larger numbers of dependants accompanied the primary applicants in certain categories. The increase over the targeted ranges for 1987 through 1990 averaged 20 per cent. For independent class immigrants, the increase reached 27 per cent in 1989 and 1 or 2 per cent more in 1990.[17] Apparently, this substantial deviation was partially due to the large numbers of dependants accompanying people in the entrepreneurial and investor categories. On average, between three and four dependants reached Canada with the primary business applicant, while in other categories the ratio of dependants to primary applicants was about one to one. These unanticipated additional arrivals contributed to the difficulties faced by public and voluntary agencies administering settlement services and raised doubts again about the credibility and usefulness of the annual intake levels process. In late 1990 Barbara McDougall, the responsible minister, stated that officials would henceforth be expected to keep the intake more in line with the announced target figures. She even suggested that the term "quota," rather than "level" or "range," might become a more accurate description of the annual exercise. Before the minister's pronouncement, officials had had no reason to restrict the processing of applications even when staff had exceeded the intake targets. In fact, regulations required officials to continue to deal with applications rather than setting them aside until the following year. Whatever social, economic, demographic, or administrative factors officials took into account when actually determining the number of immigrants desired over any one year, clearly setting targets was quite different from actually achieving them.

CONSULTATIONS WITH THE PRIVATE SECTOR

Any comprehensive examination of how annual immigrant intake levels are set must go beyond departments and agencies of the federal government. Not only the provinces but also groups in the private sector such as ethnic associations, voluntary service organizations, and the business community can all have their views heard by CEIC as it works on the annual intake levels. The process of CEIC formally consulting with a representative group of organizations on a wide range of topics, including the appropriate annual immigration levels – a requirement of the 1976 Act – began in 1980. Consultation with the rather small corps of academics who had teaching and research interests in immigration, primarily demographers, sociologists, and economists, began in 1984. Since the late 1980s the whole process has become structured, rather closed and, some observers have suggested, a little too orchestrated.[18] According to CEIC, these consultations have several objectives, including gauging informed opinion on immigration issues, providing a channel for nongovernmental input into public policy, contributing to CEIC's long-range planning capacity, and evaluating how the voluntary sector might assist with the unexpected, such as an emergency refugee movement.[19]

The origins of consulting with individuals and organizations beyond government on immigration matters can be traced to the mid-1970s, when a Special Joint Committee of the Senate and House of Commons toured Canada receiving written and oral presentations on immigration issues in preparation for the 1976 Act. The legislation provided for the establishment of an advisory council to the minister, to act as a forum for policy suggestions from outside Parliament and the bureaucracy. This body, the Canada Employment and Immigration Advisory Council, failed to fulfil its purpose, which was to perform as a dynamic voice for immigration policy innovation and evaluation. For most of its life the Advisory Council met infrequently, operated with inadequate staff to undertake research, focused more on employment than immigration issues, and had its reports and recommendations greeted with indifference by many career officials.

As a cost cutting measure, it was disbanded in 1992. Even before the council's dissolution, the responsibility of providing feedback and advice to CEIC fell to the many nongovernmental organizations in the voluntary sector and the business community. By the mid-1980s CEIC was inviting approximately 700 local, regional, and national organizations annually to comment on immigration programs, processes, and directions.[20]

The format adopted by CEIC to prepare for and carry out consultations has for some years been as follows. The commission's NHQ prepares and sends a set of background or discussion papers and similar documents, with a covering letter over the minister's signature, to hundreds of organizations and individuals. They are invited to respond to the specific proposals and general thrust of the annual immigration plan, including the intake target figures. Regional immigration officials then organize consultation sessions in major urban centres, usually in late winter or early spring, to which these groups and individuals are invited. Immigration Program officials, not only from the region but also frequently from NHQ, attend these day-long fora to explain immigration policy and regulations and to hear the views of participants.

In 1990 the consultation process changed, along with other procedures that preceded the tabling of the annual report in Parliament. The reasons for these changes were explained in the 1990 report: "This report to Parliament reflects a significant shift in the Government's approach to planning – a shift from short to long term planning, to more comprehensive consultations on immigration issues, and to a more comprehensive view of the immigration process itself."[21] To achieve such an extended projection, officials sought additional consultations with the usual groups and individuals from across Canada. During the winter and spring of 1990 twenty district and eight regional consultation meetings took place, several of which were attended by the minister.

The process of consultation means different things to different people. The rationale behind the government's approach has been to share information with interested Canadians so as to promote informed discussions and get a sense of what the voluntary and business sectors would like to see in immigration policy and practice. Some of the groups participating in this consultation process wonder just how much impact their views have when it comes to formulating or even simply amending policy and regulations. For example, as immigration level targets for 1991–95 were being tabled in Parliament, the government announced significant modifications in how dependency would be defined. Officials had made little if any mention of this proposed change during the consultations held earlier in 1990, so it came as a surprise to associations that had long lobbied for it.

The groups active in the consultation process are diverse in size, organizational structure, and degree of awareness of immigration issues. Thus, it is not possible to generalize about how these organizations see their consultative role. Their experiences, expectations, and priorities frequently differ. At the same time, it is not altogether clear how much tangible assistance in policy making the exercise can provide for Immigration Program officials, who frequently receive conflicting and contradictory input from the groups. The almost pervasive absence of any consensus among organizations in the voluntary sector enables the minister and officials to pick and choose, or even ignore, outside advice and suggestions.

In an attempt to ascertain what voluntary and other organizations believed the consultation process was intended to achieve, Immigration Program headquarters officials asked them a series of questions during 1986. Respondents were asked to indicate the most appropriate time of year for the consultation sessions, and the best format. They were also asked how they would like their views to be used by policy makers, and whether immigration policy and refugee policy issues should be dealt with separately by groups concerned with only one or the other.[22] As could have been predicted, the results of this exercise were ambiguous and unhelpful.

At best, involving hundreds of active voluntary associations encourages openness in immigration policy making. At worst, it at least provides two-way communication whereby government learns of, if not always acts on, the concerns of the private sector, and groups become aware of government priorities. Immigration officials have repeatedly tried to impress on groups that the exercise is intended to be more than a public relations operation in which the government seeks justification for policy decisions in the court of public opinion. Yet, without doubt, the consultation process does fulfil a legitimization function for the government. Despite the efforts of officials, the all-too-apparent suspicion with which many nongovernmental organizations regard immigration activities and the motives behind the consultation process persist.

Not only is there no consensus on many immigration issues, there is little common ground respecting how these associations see their role in the consultation exercise. Some organizations willingly sponsor refugees or have fee-for-service arrangements with the government to help newly arrived immigrants adjust. In return for this active involvement in immigration affairs, these associations believe their views should carry considerable weight with policy makers. Such organizations, activist and participatory in style, regularly reiterate their wish to play a part in determining the direction of policy and the nature of procedures. The infrequent attendance of the minister or the most senior ministerial lieutenants at the regional consultation sessions contributes to the suspicion among these associations that their input may not reach the highest echelons. While the director of the headquarters unit responsible for the annual levels exercise attended many regional consultations during the first decade of this process, his or her presence appears not to have conveyed the necessary aura of authority.

Other recipients of the annual package of consultation materials have a wide array of concerns, of which immigration is only one. These groups tend to be less militant on immigration issues when it comes to assertions of moral outrage, concentrating instead on points relating to their specific economic interests. Among these is the business sector, which routinely sees immigration programs as mechanisms for recruiting needed temporary or permanent workers.

Within CEIC itself, or among the several federal departments that are invited to contribute to the annual levels exercise, there is no noticeable consensus on the utility of the consultative process or, for that matter, the target figures themselves. Not surprisingly, the unit at immigration NHQ responsible for the levels has seen the consultation process as useful for achieving contact with the community beyond government and for discovering the concerns of informed opinion leaders of interest groups. Beyond this unit feelings about consultation are less focused and reflect easily identifiable, narrowly based organizational priorities and preferences.

The minister, as well as his or her advisers from outside the career public service, know the political costs and benefits that are at stake when nongovernmental organizations are given the opportunity to participate in the consultation exercise. The political well-being of the minister constitutes one of the prime considerations of these personal advisers. Meeting with the invited associations holds both promise and danger: it provides an opportunity to make points with the private and voluntary sectors but also leaves the minister and the immigration programs open to criticism. If the voluntary participants get the feeling that the consultation process is merely smoke and mirrors, their dissatisfaction will grow. Moreover, it is by no means certain that the political advisers in the minister's office are all that concerned with the planning process. The traditions of the Canadian parliamentary system, whereby ministers do not normally hold a portfolio for extended periods, result in the immediate taking precedence over the middle or long term. Any immigration plan that results from the statutorily required consultations receives minimal attention from these advisers. At the same time, the fact that meetings with nongovernmental agencies have now gone on for more than a decade has virtually institutionalized the process. It is not likely to disappear, although officials may be encouraged by their managers to spend less time on it.

Available evidence indicates, however, that federal departments make minimal use of the annual target figures, despite the promotional publicity they have received from the responsible unit at immigration NHQ. Writing to his supervisor about the less-than-enthusiastic feedback the unit had received from within CEIC and from other federal departments, the director pondered, "The replies are disappointing. It is difficult to speculate why there appears to be so little interest in what appears to us at Immigration to be such an important subject – a subject that cuts (or should cut) across virtually all aspects of federal policy."[23]

Developing an annual immigration intake figure through consultation and planning has both methodological problems and critics, as well as some proponents. It is, nevertheless, a part of the network of advisory machinery that the Immigration Program has created, initially because of the legislative requirements of the Act. I have analysed the process here primarily to demonstrate the plethora of variables that can help or hurt the setting or attainment of annual targets. A host of factors come into play, some systemic, others more idiosyncratic. Subsequent chapters enlarge upon the policy-making process.

5 Two Chronic Canadian Immigration Issues

Without much exaggeration, it could be argued that virtually all the components of Canada's immigration programs contain elements of controversy and contribute to chronic disputes. However, this chapter focuses on just two of the many elements of the immigration process that have routinely provoked debate both among officials at CEIC and DEA and among a growing number of voluntary associations. What is it about these two issues, visa policy and acquiring permanent-resident status from within Canada, that justifies singling them out for special attention in this study? Why not examine other aspects of policy that appear equally suitable, such as eligibility for employment authorization or requirements for medical and security screening? Certainly, these and other features of Canada's immigration programs have at times proved contentious and have attracted opposing points of view. However, the two policy issues examined below are particularly instructive in identifying competing philosophical outlooks and conflicting priorities within the bureaucratic establishment responsible for formulating and administering immigration policy.

The questions of what form visa policy should take and whether people should be processed for permanent residence from within Canada illustrate frequently conflicting views that favour enforcement and control on the one hand, and expediting the processing of applicants on the other. Furthermore, these two issues raise to prominence the questions of humanitarianism and compassion in connection with family reunification and asylum seekers. They also provide illustrations of bureaucratic politics and organizational behaviour in the federal departments responsible for administering Canada's immigration policy. Finally, they have occasioned such seemingly intractable discussion and negotiations among policy makers that they have achieved a certain notoriety.

Unlike many other aspects of public policy, neither of these issues can be resolved merely by acquiring additional funding: rather, they require political and philosophical answers. In the final analysis, both matters are regulatory and procedural and do not directly affect the issue of admissible classes.

VISA REQUIREMENTS

The need perceived by immigration officials to rigorously manage and control the flow of people into Canada is a recurring theme in this volume. The government and its officials, however, have striven to combine fairness with efficiency. CEIC and, between 1981 and 1992, the Immigration and Consular Affairs Bureau at DEA adopted a variety of tools, techniques, and approaches to regulate more effectively, and arguably more fairly, who could and could not enter Canada either temporarily or permanently. The method that has garnered the most support from officials at CEIC, if not always from foreign service personnel at DEA, is the visa, one of the most widely accepted devices for regulating transborder traffic. The visa resembles an entrance ticket in that it enables an individual to enter Canada after having been cleared or vetted by officials at an immigration post outside the country.

The concept of a visa has its foundation in the principles of state sovereignty, which hold that each government can decide how and when to give citizens of other countries access to its territory. Sovereignty permits governments to decide if the public interest would benefit from the entry of foreign individuals, whether for a temporary visit or for permanent settlement. Governments today offer a number of reasons for imposing visa requirements, of which the following are among the most significant.

First, estimates suggest that by the close of the 1980s, between 70 and 80 million restless people globally were in search of a new homeland, having rejected the economic, political, or social insecurity prevailing in their states of origin.[1] Visas provide a method of controlling the extremely large numbers seeking to enter other states. Second, the visa mechanism permits governments to screen out or intercept people deemed, for whatever reason, to be undesirable. States requiring visas are in a position to determine whether individuals seeking to enter the country pose any medical or security threat. Third, visa requirements allow officials to manage the flow of would-be newcomers more effectively: the mechanism ensures that individuals landing at airports or crossing at land border points have already been processed and are known to Canadian officials at foreign posts. A visa policy, in the view of many observers, goes a long way in enabling officials to know who is entering, how long visitors are permitted to remain, and when removal proceedings should commence if the individual in question has overstayed the allotted time on his or her visa.

Offsetting these apparent benefits accruing from a visa policy are political considerations that may weigh on Canada's diplomats and elected policy makers, especially if the visa policy is selectively rather than universally applied. Two in particular stand out. First, people already living in Canada who share ethnicity with individuals requiring visas may believe that the imposition of a visa requirement, if not universally applied, is discriminatory and constitutes a slur on their former homeland. The political party in power in Ottawa could lose votes if this sense of being singled out became especially intense in an ethnic group whose non-Canadian members required visas. Second, a selective visa policy may have a negative effect on how Canada is perceived by other governments: a foreign government on whose citizens the visa requirement has been imposed may see Canada's action as unnecessary at best, and unfriendly at worst. DEA officials regularly caution immigration policy makers at CEIC to move carefully when contemplating the imposition of this regulatory device, particularly when relations with the country in question may worsen as a result.

A further cost of any decision to expand visa requirements is a financial and administrative one. Either officials at overseas immigration posts have to be withdrawn from other application processing duties to administer a visa policy, or else increased resources must be allocated by Treasury Board for additional visa officers. Countries whose nationals may require a visa to enter Canada are not enumerated in the *Immigration Act*. Rather, states can be added or deleted from the list of countries simply by amending the prevailing regulations. For some years immigration and foreign service officials have debated the desirability of a universal visa policy for Canada. Discussions began during the formulation of the *Immigration Act* in the mid-1970s, and have focused on the issue of requirements for people like students and visitors, rather than for potential permanent residents, who routinely need visas. Concerns arose when growing numbers of people from countries exempted from the visa requirement began to overstay the time permitted by the regulations or to claim refugee status in the expectation of then being allowed to remain indefinitely while their cases were processed. The result was that these people short-circuited or bypassed the normal processing stages abroad, in which selection criteria would have been applied by overseas officials.

In 1976, when the current *Immigration Act* was being formulated, a memorandum prepared for cabinet pointed out that Canada had traditionally avoided introducing a broad visitor-visa program, believing it was not in the national interest. While it still appeared desirable to be generous to foreigners, many of whom were potential tourists, the memorandum acknowledged that global conditions were changing. The document set out some of the benefits that would result from extending the visa policy to cover the nationals of additional states. According to the memorandum, requiring more visitors to obtain visas at posts abroad would lessen delays at ports of entry, prevent possible embarrassment and resentment when individuals were found to be inadmissible at these ports, and could prevent adverse relationships from arising with other governments.[2]

The increase in terrorist acts around the world, combined with the fact that the Olympics were in Montreal in 1976, added extra fuel to the thrust for extended visa requirements. Moreover, officials recognized that political or economic instability in visa-exempt states could result in an overwhelming volume of unexpected and unprocessed foreigners trying to enter Canada. Historical experience and common sense, however, have dictated that Canada has never imposed a visa requirement on all states. In a memorandum, officials asserted that states should be visa-exempt where there existed a traditional relationship with Canada, close economic ties, proximity, a substantial volume of visitor traffic, and the need to use limited resources selectively.[3] For both historic and very practical reasons, officials had no desire to impose a visa requirement on United States citizens: the millions of annual border crossings by Americans ruled out any such requirement.

By the 1980s, with a marked increase in undocumented migrants making frivolous refugee status claims and people from visa-exempt Third World countries overstaying the permitted time, the visitor-visa issue took on renewed significance. However, it was one thing for CEIC officials to recommend imposing new visa requirements on visitors, but quite another to obtain the resources that would enable posts abroad to successfully administer such a policy. An illustration or two may be helpful here.

Visitors choosing to stay beyond the permitted number of days became a growing problem for immigration officials. During the late

1970s and early 1980s, nationals from India, Portugal, and Guyana ranked high among those who overstayed the period allowed for visits. When officials first suggested that visas be required from Indian citizens, the proposal was rejected, not because of strong feelings about placing a restriction on India but because the New Delhi immigration post could not obtain funds from Treasury Board to move into larger premises and hire the additional staff required to screen visa applicants.[4]

At approximately the same time, CEIC officials proposed that Portugal be placed on the list of countries whose nationals required visas. DEA officials succeeded in having the proposal set aside by arguing convincingly that, for the sake of North Atlantic Alliance (NATO) unity, Portugal must not be treated any differently from other NATO members.[5]

In the case of Guyana, again, no visa requirement was imposed because Canada had no immigration office in Georgetown and new funds would be needed if it established one there to process visa applications. But, more to the point, officials felt that an office in Guyana would encourage the flow of immigrant applications from this Third World country.[6] Only later in the 1980s, when the government's mood had become more restrictive and inflexible, did visas become mandatory for nationals of these three countries. By then the government's approach reflected fears of rising immigration fraud and abuse caused by mounting migratory pressures from a host of economically less developed countries.

CEIC officials developed a model, somewhat imprecise, to compare the costs of screening applicants for visitor visas at overseas posts with those of tracing, apprehending, and removing visitors from visa-exempt countries who had overstayed their allotted period in Canada. The objective was to prove beyond any doubt that the cost of enforcement activities within Canada declined sharply when visas became a requirement for visitors. Some immigration officials hoped to persuade their superiors that resources saved as a result of fewer illegal overstays could then be reallocated to DEA to cover the increased costs of processing visa applications at overseas offices.

CEIC data, in 1982 dollars, indicated that the average cost of processing a visa application abroad amounted to $16.40, while having to refuse entry to an individual at a Canadian port if he or she proved inadmissible cost $787.60. If an admitted visitor overstayed the allotted period and actually had to be located and appear at an inquiry in order that removal procedures could be undertaken, the cost could reach $2,078.20.[7] One not inconsiderable saving in human and financial resources with a visa requirement, officials pointed out, was that unsuccessful applicants would not be eligible to have their rejected cases heard by Canada's elaborate immigration appeal machinery. Applicants outside Canada are not entitled to have an adjudicator or inquiry review negative decisions taken by immigration officials at Canada's foreign posts.

In practice, Canada's approach to imposing visa requirements has been one of undisguised incrementalism bordering, some might suggest, on opportunism. Shared traditions or mutual alliance commitments have not consistently prevented a decision to put visa requirements in place. During the 1980s several countries, some like Canada belonging to the North Atlantic Treaty Organization or the Commonwealth, found themselves on the list of states whose nationals needed Canadian visitor visas. As a general rule, when a state's passports and similar documentation come to be frequently misused, and when its nationals top the list of immigrant control problems, Canada will soon impose a visa requirement. Advocates of the visa mechanism would impose visas in all circumstances likely to result in an unexpected flow of visitors into Canada's ports of entry. The visa is, after all, perceived as a tool for controlling or prohibiting the admission of unwanted persons. The number of countries on Canada's list varies depending on the extent of the control problem. In 1987, the nationals of approximately ninety countries needed visas.[8]

The possibility of reciprocity in visa requirements is often on the minds of policy makers. If Canada is going to inconvenience the citizens of a state, that foreign government may respond in kind to would-be visitors and tourists from Canada. Jamaica's nationals ranked very high on the list of immigration-control evaders during the 1980s. Moreover, visa-exempt Jamaican "overstays" had one of the highest crime rates of any visiting nationality. When contemplating the introduction of a visa for Jamaicans, Canadian officials wondered how such an action would be interpreted by the Kingston government. Would it be perceived as racially motivated, or discriminatory because it was not being universally applied against other Caribbean states? Would Jamaica retaliate by imposing a visa requirement on Canadians? Most immigration officials believed the latter was unlikely because Jamaica depended significantly on Canadian tourists for much-needed hard currency.[9] Indeed, Jamaica did not retaliate when Canada placed a visa requirement on its citizens.

However, in 1987 when Canada required visas from visitors travelling on Bolivian passports after a marked increase in the abuse of these documents by potential illegal immigrants, the La Paz government did mirror the Canadian move, primarily because Bolivia had little, if anything, to lose: few Canadians visited Bolivia. When

Canada placed a visa requirement on Turkish nationals in early 1987, at least some members of Turkey's Parliament denounced the decision and suggested in the press that among other things, commercial relations with Canada should be reassessed. However, Turkey did not retaliate with its own visa requirement for Canadians.

From time to time Canada has linked a visa requirement to its special humanitarian programs. When a refugee-producing situation arises in a particular country, like the ones that occurred in Guatemala, El Salvador, and Sri Lanka during the early and mid-1980s, Canada has promptly instituted a visa requirement for the nationals of that state in an attempt to prevent a self-selected movement of refugees from reaching this country. According to the CEIC policy in force during those years, "The key to implementing humanitarian immigration measures is controlling the inflow, for without controlling intake, it is not possible to constitute a pro-active set of program measures to assist those that need our help."[10] Such an approach was very much in keeping with the government's contention that the Office of the United Nations High Commissioner for Refugees (UNHCR) and Canadian visa officials overseas were in the best position to determine the level of desperation and the extent of the need of bona fide refugees. This approach rested on the belief that the ability to reach Canada did not indicate or ensure that the most endangered people were actually receiving protection. At the time prevailing official opinion held that Canada, far from refugee-producing states, should not accept undocumented people, no matter what factors had caused them to leave their homelands.

Many knowledgeable members of Canadian voluntary organizations vehemently opposed this view, arguing instead that truly frightened people, with well-founded fears of imprisonment or worse, could not afford to await the issuance of a Canadian visa by well-meaning but rigid officials.[11] As discussed elsewhere in this volume, the government's position changed publicly when the *Annual Report to Parliament on Future Immigration Levels* was tabled in October 1990. In this document the government reluctantly acknowledged that with as many as 25,000 people annually arriving at Canada's ports of entry and acquiring refugee status following an appropriate hearing, Canada had become a de facto state of first asylum. What the former policy had failed to appreciate is that all governments would like to enjoy the option of choosing who to admit as immigrants or refugees. The countries who are states of first asylum today certainly did not opt for the "privilege."

By the mid-1980s, the two issues of when and where to impose visa requirements and how to curtail the apparently uncontrolled influx to Canada of undocumented migrants claiming to be refugees had become inexorably connected in the minds of policy makers. A task force was created in 1986 to deal once and for all with how to prevent persons from entering Canada seemingly at will, while other officials addressed the issue of whether to require visas from all visitors except for residents of the United States. Officials examined the experiences other countries had had with a universal visa requirement. They found that Australia and the United States, for example, viewed the measure as not cost effective. Both governments were in the process of exploring alternatives that would be less expensive but would still protect them from abuses.[12] Officials estimated that even with Americans exempted, Canada would need to issue more than 1,500,000 visas annually, of which approximately 900,000 would be for citizens of Britain, West Germany, France, and Japan. Visitors from these states did not pose control problems. The cost of such a program would be high. During the first year that a visa requirement had been in force for Portugese citizens, the expenditures had amounted to $743,000; for the Turkish program, they had reached $260,000. While officials could not predict exactly what the total cost of a universal program would be, one estimate given to the Chairman of the House of Commons Standing Committee on Labour, Employment and Immigration placed the figure at $86,000,000.[13] Treasury Board would look exceedingly closely before approving any such expenditures.

Opposition to a broadened visa requirement has not been confined to individuals and organizations espousing humanitarian concerns. The tourism and travel industry believes that a visitor-visa requirement deters foreign travellers from coming to Canada, thus eroding profits. Prior to 1983 only a few countries' nationals needed transit visas to pass through Canada en route to other destinations. People remaining in the country for less than forty-eight hours were generally exempted from such a requirement. However, by the early 1980s this privilege was being increasingly abused; many people reached Canada and immediately entered a claim for refugee status rather than continuing their journeys. Between 1983 and 1987, Canada added eighteen countries to the list of states whose citizens required transit visas.

Canada's transportation industry has tried to have these now quite rigid transit visa requirements liberalized. Writing to the responsible minister in 1987, an executive of what was then CP Air explained: "Visa requirements adversely affect passengers from choosing Canada as a convenient link to other countries if our regulations make travel more difficult than routing through other countries ...

Canada is becoming an inhospitable environment for through service to other countries ... These are the same passengers that make it possible for Canadian airlines to operate ... competitively in other markets."[14] The letter went on to assert that there were not enough Canadians to keep transportation companies truly competitive without carrying a sizeable number of foreign nationals. Speaking for the industry, CP Air defended the record of Canada's transportation companies and requested that they be allowed to carry foreign travellers without transit visas as they had in the past. The government did not revoke the transit visa program, but did meet with representatives of the airline industry in an attempt to explain why the policy decision had been taken and to minimize its effect on their operations.

Whether to impose visas selectively or universally persists as an issue for officials. The "facilitators" would prefer to strictly limit the application of the visitor visa requirement in order to reduce the personnel needed to screen and process applications and to generally expedite the movement of visitors to Canada. The "gatekeepers," however, would prefer an extended visa program in order to regulate the type and number of people entering Canada, even for short periods, more effectively, and to reduce abuse of the normal immigrant selection and sponsorship programs. Adopting such an approach avoids surprises.

The visa is not an end in itself: it is no more than a method of managing or regulating who enters the country. In Canada, the tendency has been to adopt it selectively in reaction to an unexpected flow of persons from a specific state. The device has seldom been put in place before an unwanted rise in the rate of arrivals from a certain state has begun, or a state's travel documents have been used improperly. Possibly, if the capability of officials to predict irregular flows of humanity improved, the visa requirement could be imposed sooner. In the final analysis, any decision to adopt a universal visa requirement will be determined by managerial, financial, and security considerations. Governments will spend the needed money if, in their view, the welfare of the state may be in jeopardy. Not until those favouring universal visa programs have made their case successfully will the decision to impose one be taken.

APPLICATIONS FOR PERMANENT RESIDENCE FROM WITHIN CANADA

As with visa policy, the question whether potential immigrants should be permitted to apply for permanent residence from within

Canada, rather than only at Canadian posts abroad, has given rise to much debate within and between CEIC and DEA. Like visa policy, the applications-in-Canada issue brings a number of chronic, underlying concerns to the surface. These include how best to control who settles in Canada, where humanitarianism and compassion fit into the administration of immigration policy, and what procedures are suitable for facilitating the annual immigration intake. While such questions are by no means confined to this particular problem, it is on this topic that bureaucratic divisions have become especially pronounced.

To appreciate the issue's complexity and emotive character, some background is necessary. During the mid-1960s, Canada made major alterations in its immigration policy and regulations to remove the last vestiges of official ethnic discrimination and to introduce the universal point system governing eligibility. As described in an earlier chapter, this meant that applicants for permanent residence needed to attain a certain number of points, which were awarded for things such as language skills, education, age, and relatives already living in Canada. People already in Canada temporarily, such as visitors, students, or temporary workers, could also apply for this landed status from within the country. Not all applicants, of course, were successful. By 1972, tens of thousands of rejected applications for landed status had created an enormous backlog in the protracted appeals process, causing the government to cancel the provisions enabling individuals to apply from within Canada.

The practice of receiving landed status from within Canada, however, did not halt at all. Since Regulation 34, the regulation permitting people to become landed from within Canada, was rescinded in 1972 a substantial number of people have been allowed to remain each year. For example, in 1975 16,800 individuals were able to stay because they received minister's permits, a procedure by which officials at inland offices can grant permission to remain in the country.[15] This was not by any means an aberration. Even after the present *Immigration Act*, which explicitly requires applicants to be screened and visaed at posts outside Canada, came into force in 1978, the number of people who initially entered the country with some temporary status and were then allowed to remain continued to be significant. During the early to mid-1980s, the numbers receiving minister's permits regularly constituted approximately 20 per cent of the total annual arrivals.[16] The majority of those availing themselves of this officially abnormal route have been members of the family class, chiefly spouses and dependent children who have acquired landed status under the humanitarian and compassionate provisions of the Act.

Inland immigration officials had a certain range of discretion with respect to these provisions. In some instances where, in the view of officials, humanitarian or compassionate reasons were absent, applicants for landed status could still travel to the nearest Canadian immigration post in the United States to obtain a visa. This procedure, called the "Buffalo shuffle," was made possible by the negotiation of an agreement between the American and Canadian governments. The agreement allowed the applicant to temporarily enter the United States in order to visit the Canadian immigration post and acquire the necessary documentation before returning immediately to Canada. Such permission was granted when "if special action were not taken, Canadian citizens and permanent residents might suffer loss of employment, financial reverses, lack of education, impaired health services or the deterioration of the spiritual needs of their community."[17] The purpose of the regulation was to limit the disruption to Canadians and their religious, educational, financial, or commercial interests. In practice, people found to be bona fide refugees by Canada's status determination machinery have also been granted permanent residence from within the country. During the mid- and late 1980s, the numbers having their situations regularized through the refugee status determination process reached into the thousands annually. Other categories of people who have been allowed to change from temporary to permanent status without first leaving Canada to do so include foreign domestics who have been employed for two continuous years and people who initially came here as visitors or students but have been permitted through special measures programs to remain because of refugee-producing circumstances or civil unrest in their homelands.

What constitutes justifiable humanitarian or compassionate reasons for permitting applicants to acquire landed immigrant status from within Canada has been difficult to determine. While guidelines are helpful, immigration managers at inland offices have frequently found the volume of applications for permanent residence overwhelming. Officials have not been permitted by their supervisors, however, to make blanket offers of permanent status for the personal convenience of their clients. Certainly, individuals who have had their applications for permanent residence rejected at overseas posts can not expect to acquire such status at offices within Canada.

Depiste the thousands who do attain permanent residence from within Canada, a strong preference for overseas processing has persisted among control-minded immigration personnel. Reality, however, forces these same officials to recognize that awarding permanent residence to some individuals already in Canada will continue to be unavoidable. A memo prepared by Calvin Best, then executive director of the Immigration Branch early in the life of the present Act, expresses this feeling most cogently.

It would be preferable to process such [family class] applications overseas in order to more easily identify fraudulent applications and since processing abroad is more efficient in terms of resources and the time required. While the better management of the immigration movement could be achieved by requiring that all such applications be made abroad, the humanitarian and compassionate considerations that are frequently involved and the lack of a telling reason for forcing the applicant to leave Canada, make it unrealistic for the Commission to force all such ... applicants to make their request for permanent residence from abroad.[18]

Officials have constantly been concerned about the possibility of applicants providing fraudulent information. This fear surfaced when it was suggested that the spouses of people already in Canada might be permitted to apply for residence from within the country, a possibility under the humanitarian and compassionate provisions of the *Immigration Act*. During the early 1980s the term "marriages of convenience" appeared with increasing regularity in officials' conversations and correspondence. Such marriages were defined as undertakings to ensure an applicant's ability to remain in Canada when all other channels for acquiring landed status had been exhausted. However, a ruling of the Supreme Court of Canada in 1983, *Robbins v. Canada (Minister of Employment and Immigration)*, prevented officials from using a suspected marriage of convenience as a reason for excluding a spouse otherwise eligible for landed status.

Through the mid-1980s, the issue of acquiring permanent residence from within Canada became caught up in at least two difficult questions. From where in the immigration establishment would discretionary decisions emanate? On what sort of guidelines would such discretion rest? Management at immigration N H Q continued to prefer guidelines over actual fixed regulations to govern the handling of applications from within Canada. Yet, interpretations of these guidelines could and did vary from region to region.

These questions arose as a result of larger, unresolved problems concerning the appropriate degree of decentralization within the Immigration Program. The situation became less confused when the

Federal Court handed down a decision stating that officials were "bound" to consider all requests from people within Canada for the waiving of external processing requirements. This judicial ruling allowed officials, acting on behalf of their minister, to determine which cases warranted foreign visa processing exemptions. To expedite decisions, the Federal Court instructed in *Perez v. Canada (Minister of Employment and Immigration)* that the authority to grant visa exemptions be kept at the examining officer level, as administrative fairness was more likely at this point in the organizational hierarchy.[19] Immigration NHQ had held the view that if the interviewing official decided to reject a request for a visa waiver, the official should refer the case to his or her supervisor. Moreover, the same process should be followed when the junior officer was confronted by controversial or politically sensitive cases. The judicial ruling did not resolve the broader question of how decentralized immigration operatons should become.

In 1986 immigration NHQ established a Special Projects Unit to focus, among other things, on how delivery of the immigration program could be streamlined. The objective was to enable increased numbers of people to resettle in Canada without requiring Treasury Board to provide funding for additional processing personnel. One approach to solving this puzzle involved once again examining the costs and benefits of increased use of applications from within Canada. The contentiousness of the issue had not diminished over the years since the 1976 *Immigration Act* had been formulated, but few new arguments were advanced on either side. In an effort to reach a consensus once and for all on what to do about this all-too-apparent inconsistency between de jure and de facto practices, the unit's director drafted a comprehensive discussion paper to elicit responses from officials both at headquarters and in the field. As was to be expected with such a contentious issue, responses to the paper were divided.

The discussion paper opened by stating the nub of the matter. "A cornerstone of Canada's immigration policy is the Act's intent that persons should make their applications abroad. At present, this intent does not coincide with practice as persons are able to apply and receive landed immigrant status from within Canada. Even though it may be an awkward and cumbersome procedure to have to do from within, still it is resorted to frequently."[20] The paper thus pointed out the not inconsequential difference between what was publicly asserted as policy and what was actually done, a divergence that confused not only sponsors and applicants but officials as well.

The paper, in the final analysis, came down on the side of regularizing landings from within Canada. It argued that the door to universal access would not swing open if limited regularization for spouses and dependants, part of the family class, was implemented. The responses prepared by the opponents of regularization pointed to a number of factors, all of which had been debated in the past. For example, it was argued that the identities of people claiming to be eligible for admission under family class provisions could be verified more accurately by visa officials in the countries from which these individuals were emigrating. Thus, spurious family class applications were less likely to go undetected. Moreover, should family class applications be processed within Canada, rejected applicants or their sponsors would be quite within their rights to launch actions before the Immigration Appeals Board, thereby extending the process and conceivably creating backlogs like those that encumbered the refugee status determination machinery.

While the protracted debate proceeded, thousands of people applying for permanent status from within Canada continued to be processed. Even the possibility of receiving landed status from within Canada was enough to inspire applicants and would-be sponsors to enter the process. Moreover, the word spread as immigration consultants and lawyers advised clients to at least try this channel of admission. Any chance of success from within the country proved to be more attractive than entering the screening process from abroad.

The work of the Special Project Unit came to a halt in the spring of 1988 as immigration NHQ went through another of several reorganizations. As the activity in the unit wound down, its director, reporting to J.B. Bissett, then executive director of the Immigration Program, acknowledged that the issue of applications from within Canada had not been resolved. The report concluded by expressing the view that if family class applicants were to be processed regularly from within the country, redeployment of personnel from DEA to inland Canadian Immigration Centres would be necessary, involving many complexities. Without additional staff, regularization from within Canada would strain the capacity of domestic immigration operations too severely.[21] As of the close of 1990, neither CEIC officials nor the minister had produced any conclusive answer to this ongoing question. Meanwhile thousands of minister's permits are used annually to grant spouses and dependants landed immigrant status from within Canada.

After this detailed description of the visa and landings-within-Canada issues, what conclusions can be drawn? These two issues provide useful illustrations of phenomena that have and continue to shape policy. Officials favouring something approaching a universal visa requirement and rigid, explicit limits on granting landed status from within Canada work very much from the traditional "gate-keeper" mind-set. This high priority on control is apparent in many, conceivably most, regulatory agencies or bodies charged with managing the flow of measurable items, whether they be people or inanimate commodities. Those bureaucrats and their political masters who display this strong urge for control would remove most if not all opportunity for people to select themselves as immigrants and future permanent residents. Advocates of extended regulation argue with conviction that selection criteria appear in the legislation and regulations and should constitute the exclusive yardstick for evaluating applicants wishing to resettle in Canada.

A somewhat different view of these issues can be found among other officials and political leaders, just as earnest about fulfilling the objectives of Canada's immigration legislation. This mind-set, more inclined to emphasize facilitation and the importance of expediting applicant processing, reflects more confidence in the ultimate value of would-be immigrants who, on their own initiative, seek out Canada. Proponents of this point of view, while not condoning the flouting of regulations and institutionalized procedures, nevertheless tend, in the final analysis, to have faith in the contribution these people can make to Canadian society. Just as the gatekeepers can be criticized for their exclusionist tendencies, the facilitators can be perceived as being naïve and blindly optimistic about human nature. This dichotomy is apparent in the debate surrounding the two issues discussed in this chapter.

6 Canada's Refugee Policy: A Conundrum

Of all the elements of Canada's immigration policy, those relating to the admission of refugees were the most controversial and criticized. They also caused severe administrative and managerial problems during the 1980s. Canadian refugee policy could quite easily sustain a book length analysis rather than merely being the focus of two chapters. This and the following chapter explain the nature of Canada's refugee policy and programs as they have evolved since the late 1970s, examine the factors and forces within and beyond government that have influenced them, and discuss the obstacles that over the years have impeded their prompt, effective implementation.

As the opening chapter of this study states, most human migration has stemmed from the belief that conditions elsewhere promised more material satisfaction. Migration in these instances was voluntary and possibly even well planned. What ultimately distinguishes these migrants from refugees are the reasons precipitating their moves. Refugees feel compelled to flee from their habitual surroundings, believing their lives or freedom are threatened by actions taken or condoned by the state. A well-founded fear of persecution because of race, religion, or political opinion frequently drives people to seek sanctuary in a country other than the one in which they have previously resided. Refugees can no longer feel safe in their homelands, and mistrust the protection of their former states.[1]

THE DEVELOPMENT OF CANADA'S
REFUGEE POLICY

For most of Canada's immigration history, neither politicians nor officials made any distinction between immigrants and refugees. The reasons for people's departures from their homelands seldom interested officials responsible for processing those who wanted to settle in Canada. Instead, migrants from abroad were looked at for what they had to offer in terms of satisfying labour market needs, supplying capital and know-how for job-creating projects, or simply settling the land. Without doubt, a portion of those who settled in Canada as early as the closing years of the eighteenth century would, by today's definitions, be described as refugees. For example, many of what have come to be known as United Empire Loyalists felt compelled to leave the embryonic American republic in search of a way of life more in keeping with the values and traditions of the British Crown. Using present-day definitions, other identifiable refugee groups settling in Canada before World War II included fugitive slaves and Hutterites from the United States, Mennonites and Doukhobors from Czarist Russia, and Jews from Eastern Europe.

Not until the passage of the 1976 *Immigration Act* did refugees as such constitute an admissible class for resettlement. As pointed out in chapter 3, members of the refugee class enjoy the same high priority when being processed as do applicants from the family class. In the three decades between the resumption of immigration to Canada after World War II and the coming into force of the present Act in 1978, special refugee admission schemes were only made possible with the passage of orders in council, which suspended normal immigration regulations and routines and permitted relaxed criteria for screening and processing to be substituted. Among the groups that benefited from relaxed regulations during this thirty-year period were approximately 165,000 East European displaced persons who came in the immediate postwar years, 38,000 Hungarians who fled following the failure of a liberal uprising in their homeland in 1956, 11,000 Czechs and Slovaks who left after the demise of a reform movement in their homeland in 1968, 7,000 Ugandan Asians who were expelled from Uganda by then President Idi Amin in the early 1970s, and a similar number of Chileans who left after the violent seizure of power by the country's military in 1973.[2] During those thirty years over 300,000 refugees, primarily Europeans, resettled in Canada as a result of relaxed regulatory provisions. The current Act, with its recognition of Canada's international obligations and humanitarian traditions, ensures a basic level of compassionate treatment for refugees as defined in the 1951 Convention Relating to the Status of Refugees.

The 1976 *Immigration Act* also provides for a designated class category to be applied, when the cabinet sees fit, to persons who are not refugees in the strict sense of the definition but who find themselves in refugee-like situations. This classification has been invoked to permit the entry to Canada under relaxed criteria of persons from regions and countries such as Indo-China, Eastern Europe, Lebanon, and Chile.

The 1976 legislation permitted for the first time private sponsorship of refugees and members of designated classes by service clubs, church congregations, and nongovernmental organizations generally. Private sponsors were required to guarantee support of an individual or a refugee family for one year. The plan envisaged the sponsors ensuring that refugees had adequate food and shelter, and were being helped to find employment and to adjust to life in a new, culturally different, country. The legislation made it possible, or even desirable in the view of officials, for nationally based nongovernmental organizations to sign umbrella refugee sponsorship arrangements with Ottawa. Formal agreements with such national bodies identified the organization as the guarantor of obligations undertaken by local affiliates or chapters wishing to sponsor government-selected refugees. Such contracts went far to remove some of the financial anxiety felt by many local groups that were otherwise quite prepared to accept the significant responsibility for an individual or family of refugees.

The private sponsorship approach achieved its greatest popularity among local groups during 1979 and 1980, at the height of the massive exodus from the Indo-Chinese states. Sponsoring came to be so widespread among Canadians, most of whom were novices when it came to first-hand contact with people from foreign cultures, that new liaison positions in Canada Immigration Centres were established across the country to help groups carry out their responsibilities to refugees.

In addition, the Act also contained provisions for determining the status of persons claiming to be refugees who had reached Canadian ports of entry without previously being screened and processed by overseas visa officials. How to deal with claims for refugee status by people already in Canada has proved the most acrimonious feature of immigration policy since the passage of the 1976 Act, and is considered fully in the next chapter.

As the foregoing paragraphs suggest, Canada's refugee admissions policy contains two quite distinct components. The first, the provisions officials expected to be used most, related to overseas selection, by visa officials, of government or privately sponsored refugees, carried out in states where these refugees have found temporary sanctuary. The second, the provisions that became so politically and administratively awkward and controversial, concerned people already in Canada making claims for refugee status, without having been previously processed or issued with travel documents. To some observers, this second set of provisions marked Canada as a state of first asylum, a label immigration officials persistently rejected until the early 1990s. Only with the publication by CEIC in 1990 of the *Report on the 1991–1995 Immigration Levels Consultations* did Canada acknowledge this status. The report declared, "It should be emphasized ... that Canada is now a country of first asylum, a country to which refugees look first for protection."[3]

Each autumn, in the annual report to Parliament on future immigration levels, the number of Convention refugees and designated class members expected to enter Canada during the subsequent year is announced. From time to time during the 1980s CEIC produced three-year projections of the overall immigration intake to assist provincial and municipal government agencies and the voluntary sector in planning their immigrant adjustment programs, but those figures excluded refugees. Explaining this omission, the 1981 report to Parliament stated, "It is not realistic ... to attempt a precise forecast of refugee and designated class intake for a period of more than one year because of the volatile nature of the international refugee situation."[4]

That practice changed with the tabling in Parliament of the immigration plan for 1991 through 1995 in October 1990. This document contained multiyear projections for the number of refugees and designated class members expected both to be processed abroad and to be granted refugee status from within Canada. To be sure, given the frequently unpredictable nature of global political situations, projections for more than one year remain little more than educated guesses on the part of even veteran officials. Generally, throughout the 1980s, the annual estimate for refugee and designated class intake reflected the number of applicants overseas visa officials could process, the volume of refugee claimants expected to have their status regularized within Canada, the number of groups prepared to initiate private sponsorship activities, and the overall capacity of governmental and private agencies to help persons resettle smoothly in Canada.

Estimates suggest that during the first half of the 1990s, approximately 13,000 government-sponsored refugees – people selected by overseas visa officials who will receive financial support from CEIC to help them adapt – will be brought to Canada annually. Thousands more will be privately sponsored annually or will have their claims for refugee status affirmed by the Immigration and Refugee Board (discussed in chapter 7) from within the country. Officials responsible for formulating Canada's refugee policy feel that, in the future, more emphasis will be placed on selecting people who are in critical need of protection. These will be refugees, or people in refugee-like situations, who are known or at least believed to be in life-threatening predicaments. An example of such a crisis would be threats by a state to forcibly return individuals to the country from which they have just escaped, an act referred to by jurists as *refoulement*. In the past, Canada has been expected by agencies such as UNHCR to concentrate on settling substantial numbers of refugees in an effort to lessen the congestion often present in overcrowded and unsafe holding centres in states of first asylum. It may be that in the 1990s Canada's overseas refugee selection efforts will place less emphasis on total numbers and more on potential *refoulement* situations, as well as on people otherwise in the greatest need.

To illustrate, women and girls make up the majority in many refugee camps in Africa and Asia. The males have often been detained by authorities or killed in outbreaks of violence. Female refugees may well find themselves exposed to extreme sexual harassment or worse by soldiers and guards, who may control medical supplies and food distribution to the refugees. Canada could conceivably select a larger portion of its annual intake from this particularly vulnerable segment of the refugee population.[5]

Throughout the mid-1970s when the 1976 *Immigration Act* was being drafted, and afterwards, CEIC officials have adamantly asserted that the refugee definition adopted by Canada should be rigid, remaining true to the letter and spirit of the definition contained in the 1951 Convention.[6] Rather than broadening the legislated definition when extraordinary international circumstances warranted new compassionate assistance programs, these officials believed it would be preferable to use the provisions for temporarily creating designated classes. A too-liberal legal definition could attract an ever-increasing flood of anguished migrants and result in unwanted control problems for the immigration machinery.

A smaller group of immigration officials, along with a segment of foreign service officers at DEA, called for continued or even increased Canadian activity to lessen the severity of refugee situations. A paper proposing a strategy for Canada in this area expressed the following belief: "The persistence and frequency of refugee outflows and the fact that third country resettlement is not a viable solution for most of these crises suggests that while Canada should continue to play an important role in settling refugees where this form of help is needed, our expertise, our international objectives and the strength of Canadian public commitment to this cause all suggest that we could, and should, provide leadership in meeting the more complex and major refugee crises now facing the international community."[7] In another strategy paper, officials from DEA pursued this internationalist line of thought still further. The paper focused on officials' growing concern about human rights infractions in states of first asylum. It went on to urge the government, when discussing refugee phenomena with other governments, to encourage additional planning for private sponsorship of refugees on a worldwide basis, and pressed the view that Canada act, and be seen to act, as a viable interlocutor among different regional and ideological groupings of states involved with refugees.[8] In general these and other memoranda that proposed policy zeroed in on possible strategies for emergency relief assistance, protection, resettlement, and the root causes of refugee movements. Canada's policy then and now is frequently described by its formulators as reflecting a humanitarian and compassionate approach that should not be seen as aimed exclusively at refugees but as encompassing a broader spectrum of people in real need. The designated class provisions of the immigration legislation make this flexibility possible. The estimated 70 to 80 million people on the move around the world, in various stages of desperation, demand some level of attention from governments. In many instances these people left their states of origin to escape social, environmental, economic, and political conditions not of their own making. Yet they are not political refugees in the strict sense of the Convention's definition.[9] As difficult as the circumstances for these millions of people are, the vast majority are not in immediate physical danger. Still, their plight cries out for attention and fuels the debate over how rigid or flexible refugee definitions should be. Meanwhile, the question whether these "economic refugees" should be assisted by the international community remains unanswered.

Anxiety in Canada and elsewhere over the rise in the practice of *refoulement*, the act of involuntary repatriation, mounted in the years under analysis here. This erosion of concern for the protection of bona fide refugees has worried UNHCR; more *refoulement* cases are reported every year. While the increase has not been confined to any one region of the world, during the 1980s it became especially apparent in Central America and sub-Saharan Africa.

Throughout the first half of the 1980s, both unilaterally and in concert with other like-minded states, Canada pursued what can quite accurately be described as a humane, enlightened course of action towards refugees and distressed people. The Canadian government worked within the diplomatic apparatus of UNHCR to search out durable solutions to refugee situations and to provide emergency relief as crises emerged. At the same time, between 17,000 and 20,000 refugees and members of designated classes arrived in Canada annually under government and private sponsorship programs. Between 1980 and 1987, approximately 25 per cent of these arrivals were Convention refugees, while the overwhelming majority came under the temporary designated classes established from time to time by order in council.[10]

In recognition of these efforts and accomplishments in the field of refugee assistance, Canada was awarded the Nansen Medal by UNHCR in a ceremony at Ottawa in November 1986. On no other occasion has an entire country received this honour. An examination of the more significant refugee and quasi-refugee movements in which Canada has played a significant role, and which contributed to the awarding of the medal, follows.

INDO-CHINA

Of all the humanitarian admissions programs initiated by Canada since the 1976 *Immigration Act* came into force, that admitting people from the Indo-Chinese states proved to be the largest and longest. Following the fall of Saigon to the North Vietnamese forces and the reunification of Vietnam in 1975, an ever increasing flow of former South Vietnamese left their country, either by land or in overcrowded, unseaworthy boats. This exodus became a torrent in the closing years of the 1970s. At the same time other sizeable movements of humanity were getting underway from Laos and Cambodia. Hundreds of thousands of desperate but unwanted people reached Thailand, Malaysia, and other Southeast Asian states in search of a new life. The already economically overextended governments of these reluctant states of first asylum were both unwilling and unable to cope with this onslaught of humanity and called on UNHCR and other international agencies and national governments to assist in resettling the Indo-Chinese elsewhere.

The appeal of the "boat people" reached its zenith for the Western media in 1979 and 1980, arousing enormous sympathy among the Canadian public. In an unprecedented demonstration of generosity, service clubs, church congregations, neighbourhood associations, and spontaneously organized groups of families eagerly embarked on private sponsorship of more than 25,000 people during 1979 alone and continued this activity, on a smaller scale, well into the 1980s. The Canadian government sponsored still larger numbers. Thousands of Vietnamese have continued to gain admission annually. The Indo-Chinese initially qualified for entry to Canada under the designated class provisions of the *Immigration Act* because they did not fit the more rigid definition of a refugee in the 1951 Convention. Since the peak period for arrivals, the Indo-Chinese already in Canada have sponsored thousands of their family members under the relevant immigration legislation and regulations. From a high point of more than 60,000 who reached Canada from states of temporary asylum in Southeast Asia during 1979 and 1980, the number of arrivals has levelled off at under 10,000 annually.[11]

Even before the post-1975 movement, small numbers of Vietnamese had begun to come to Canada with the introduction of the universal admissions approach and the point system in the late 1960s. As many spoke French, they were seen by the province of Quebec as especially desirable newcomers. The influx of Indo-Chinese during and after 1979 made the earlier Vietnamese arrivals appear inconsequential in comparison. Vietnamese sheltering in nearby states made up the majority of those selected for resettlement in Canada, but they by no means constituted the entire movement. Laotians and Cambodians also joined the queue, hoping to be selected for processing and documentation by teams of Canadian immigration officials working in refugee centres in Thailand, Malaysia, and neighbouring countries.

In 1977, to the surprise of Canadian authorities, the Vietnamese government suggested that it would be appropriate to have some of its nationals reunited with relatives already in Canada. This early attempt, serious or half-hearted, by the Hanoi government to establish orderly departure mechanisms for some of those wishing to emigrate was quite another matter from the massive unmanaged exodus then overwhelming several states in Southeast Asia. The Vietnamese government proposed that it manage the selection of individuals through its own authority to issue exit visas. However, Canadian officials were not prepared to surrender the right to choose who should enter Canada. Vietnamese authorities, on their part, reacted equally negatively to Ottawa's suggestion that Canadian medical and security personnel who normally worked out of Hong Kong visit Hanoi to interview applicants and conduct medical screening.[12]

Despite their misgivings, Hanoi and Ottawa did not close the door on further discussions. The Vietnamese family reunification program ultimately began at the close of the 1970s but was not without problems. Even though UNHCR worked with the Canadian and other interested Western governments to promote orderly departures from Vietnam, numerous obstacles placed in the way of the smooth movement of people by Hanoi plagued the scheme throughout its life. When functioning as planned, the program had Vietnamese already in Canada apply to immigration authorities to sponsor their relatives. Canadian officials, working through Vietnamese government offices, then tried to locate the individuals to be sponsored, and undertook preliminary processing. How soon the sponsored person arrived in Canada ultimately depended on the speed of the exit visa process within the Vietnamese bureaucracy.

From time to time, Vietnamese officials reiterated the view that only people designated under their procedures, rather than those selected by Canadian officials based on sponsor requests, should emigrate. Canada consistently rejected this proposal even when faced by threats to suspend the issuing of exit permits entirely. Hanoi regularly sought to use Canada's family reunification program as a wedge to enable independent unsponsored nationals without connections in Canada to immigrate here.[13]

As the 1980s proceeded the backlog of applications from anxious Vietnamese sponsors in Canada increased. By March 1982 the number of sponsor applications requiring attention had reached approximately 11,000.[14] For every application processed during that year, four more were received. At the close of 1982 the backlog had climbed to 31,000, while the Vietnamese government had only issued 2,000 exit visas, which were a prerequisite of departure.[15]

The objective of the orderly departures from Vietnam negotiated by Western governments and UNHCR was to relieve the crowded, overextended states of Southeast Asia of their unwanted "guests." In 1984, for the first time since the mass exodus of Indo-Chinese had begun in the previous decade, the collective actions of members of the international community resulted in the number of people leaving Vietnam in orderly departures exceeding those arriving on their own in neighbouring states. In that same year, Vietnamese nationals constituted the largest group immigrating to Canada.[16] Between the beginning of the orderly departure program in 1979 and the close of 1985, approximately 22,000 people reached Canada directly from Vietnam.[17] An additional 2,300 arrived in 1986 and similar numbers arrived through the remainder of the decade. At the same time, Canada continued to accept somewhat smaller numbers of Indo-Chinese who had temporarily been accommodated in other Southeast Asian states.

What set this Vietnamese family class program apart from other Canadian sponsorship schemes was the difficulty immigration officials encountered in fulfilling the processing requirements. Vietnamese authorities routinely acted inconsistently and erratically, frequently hindering rather than helping Canadian attempts to locate the relatives of Vietnamese sponsors already in Canada. Considering the circumstances, the substantial numbers that did enter Canada from Vietnam through this program are rather astounding.

POLAND

Before the Indo-Chinese movement to Canada began, Eastern Europe had been the source of most Convention refugees and members of designated classes accepted into Canada. Since the late 1940s tens of thousands of Eastern Europeans from countries then within the Soviet Union's sphere of influence had gained entry to Canada, beginning with the displaced persons of the postwar era. Following the rise of the Solidarity movement in Poland in 1980–81 and the imposition of martial law by the Polish government in late 1981, Canada put in place a program specifically for citizens of that country.

Both foreign and domestic political factors contributed to this Canadian initiative. The foreign policy objective of the plan was to relieve Austria, the state providing sanctuary to the majority of exiting Poles, of the inordinate burden of these unexpected new arrivals. For decades Austria had acted as the gateway to the West and principal state of first asylum for Eastern Europeans fleeing politically oppressive and economically depressed conditions. The domestic political motive came from Canadians of Polish extraction, who pressed the government to introduce special measures to assist friends and relatives seeking prompt access to Canada as conditions in Poland worsened.

In October 1981 the Canadian government announced that Poles already in this country on student or visitor visas would be permitted to remain here for at least one year. At the same time officials asserted that processing of applicants being sponsored by Canadian citizens or permanent residents would be expedited. The Department of External Affairs, which had only acquired responsibility for overseas immigration processing operations earlier that same year, expressed two concerns as these special measures were announced. First, expectations among the Canadian Polish community had been raised and there might be political costs if the promised rapid processing of sponsored applicants did not materialize. DEA also feared that the

Polish government might close its frontiers and stop issuing exit visas to the growing numbers of Poles wishing to emigrate.[18]

In most instances, the special Canadian measures for Poles already in Canada operated smoothly; these individuals were screened and processed at inland Canada Immigration Centres and received their permanent residence status accordingly. Like Eastern Europeans generally, these latest arrivals were not classed as Convention refugees but instead were deemed eligible for permanent residence as "self-exiles" under the designated class provisions of the legislation.

Most of the Poles seeking to leave their troubled country in these years had not been singled out for persecution by the Communist Party or the military. For the most part, they were simply trying to escape the economic deprivation and political turmoil that were rampant and still worsening. There were, however, some Poles who had been detained by authorities as a result of their known or suspected political activities. Such persons closely resembled genuine refugees except that they had not left the country of their nationality, a requirement of the formal Convention definition.

Prior to the events in Poland Canada had established a program for "political prisoners and oppressed persons" in the late 1970s, under the designated class provisions of the *Immigration Act*. This special program was initially aimed at securing the release of people detained by the Chilean and Argentinian authorities. After protracted negotiations between the Polish authorities and the Canadian embassy at Warsaw, a similar program became operational in Poland in late 1982.[19] During the first two years of this program, 599 detainees and their dependants were released and granted exit permits by Polish authorities and issued with entry visas by Canadian embassy personnel.[20] Canada extended the program for one-year periods through 1988. Meeting the annual target of 125 people proved to be difficult. In many instances of internees being released from detention, considerable time elapsed before they actually emigrated. Many hoped that the political and economic climate in Poland would change, making emigration unnecessary.

The decision by Poles to leave their homeland often crystallized gradually rather than suddenly as was usual for bona fide refugees. One Canadian official posted in Warsaw wrote, "Most applicants are prompted to apply finally for immigration to Canada because the economic picture in Poland has greatly deteriorated since 1981 and shows few signs of speedy recovery. In a climate of economic depression and little chance for personal advancement, ... it is not unusual to look elsewhere for improved living conditions."[21]

The special Canadian measures for "self-exiles" from Poland resulted in 19,826 individuals being permitted to remain in or enter Canada between October 1981 and the close of 1984.[22] During succeeding years Poles have continued to immigrate to Canada, but since the legalization of Solidarity and the liberalization of the Polish political system their admission has not fallen under the designated class provisions. Neither the Indo-Chinese nor the early Polish movements to Canada were formally considered to be influxes of Convention refugees. They were seen by the Canadian government as movements of people in refugee-like situations and were primarily administered as admissions of designated classes.

CENTRAL AMERICA

In addition to tens of thousands of people from Southeast Asia and Eastern Europe, Canada has received Convention refugees and other people covered by the designated class provisions from states in the Western hemisphere. The latter movements, also during the 1980s, came primarily from Central America. Canada's programs for refugees from El Salvador, Nicaragua, and Guatemala have been much smaller than the admission schemes for the Indo-Chinese and Poles. The country's plans to assist Central American refugees took shape rather slowly, almost reluctantly, compared with other schemes for refugees or people in refugee-like situations. Among the factors that account for this less-than-enthusiastic beginning were an absence in Canada of a Latin American community of any size or political significance, a low level of awareness among Canadians generally about events in the Western hemisphere south of the United States, and a distinct wish on the part of the Canadian government not to be seen as intervening in any way in events in what has traditionally been perceived as America's backyard.

In the late 1970s and early 1980s mounting civil unrest accompanied by increasing violence, first in Nicaragua and then in El Salvador and Guatemala, resulted in upward of 300,000 frightened people fleeing their homelands in search of safety in Honduras, Costa Rica, Mexico, and the United States. After considerable pressure from Canadian churches and other humanitarian organizations the government announced a special program in March 1981, enabling students and visitors from El Salvador who were in Canada to remain indefinitely beyond the expiry date of their visas. Subsequently citizens of El Salvador with family members already in Canada were given priority in processing when they applied to immigrate. In 1984 the government announced similar provisions for Guatemalans.

The numbers of Convention refugees processed by Canadian visa officers at posts in Central America and Mexico remained comparatively small. When Canadian churches, labour unions, academic organizations, and Amnesty International urged authorities to bring more refugees from this region to Canada, the official response remained cautious, ostensibly so as not to undercut the objectives and plans of UNHCR. Since the start of its operations in the region at the outset of the 1980s, this UN agency had preferred to see displaced Central Americans resettled temporarily and locally, in culturally similar surroundings, rather than in distant third countries. UNHCR officials hoped that conditions in the troubled states of the area would soon give way to calm and political tranquillity, thereby allowing repatriation. Agency officials counselled that resettlement in far-away states should be used as a solution only for people known to be in genuine physical danger if they remained in the region. UNHCR's plan envisaged refugees being temporarily accommodated in specially created holding centres in the rural parts of Honduras, Costa Rica, and Mexico, in surroundings not unlike those they had left behind. Speaking in Parliament in late 1981 Lloyd Axworthy, Canada's minister of employment and immigration, defended the policy of limited refugee admissions from Central America by pointing to the preferences of UNHCR. The minister explained that as so much of Canada's refugee policy was established only after consultation with the UN agency, Canada did not wish to contradict the advice and guidance given to member governments.[23] Canada's position was elaborated in the 1982 report to Parliament on future immigration levels: "The Canadian resettlement strategy in Central America is focused upon those refugees who are unlikely to be repatriated and who have a close connection in Canada, and has been developed in close cooperation with UNHCR and the Canadian churches."[24] Few Central Americans, however, had "a close connection" in Canada.

In both 1981 and 1982 CEIC's annual refugee plan projected that approximately one thousand Central Americans would arrive, but in neither year was this estimate met. When designated class provisions were applied to citizens of El Salvador in 1983, and were extended to Guatemalans one year later, the number of arrivals did increase somewhat.

As it had with Polish and Chilean authorities earlier, Canada negotiated the establishment of a "political prisoners and oppressed persons" program with the Salvadoran government, again only after concerned humanitarian and religious interest groups had put considerable pressure on Ottawa. By early 1984, 296 detainees plus their dependants had gained release from prison and were on their way to Canada.[25]

Canadian interest groups proved more active in urging generous, liberalized programs on the government in this Central American crisis than in any other refugee-producing situation during the period covered here. Still, the numbers remained small when compared with other movements discussed above.

Christian organizations such as the Inter-Church Committee on Refugees and the Inter-Church Committee on Human Rights in Latin America acquired first-hand information on the conditions of thousands of endangered Central Americans through Canadian missionaries in the field and the network provided by the World Council of Churches. These voluntary organizations may very well have had more accurate, up-to-date information through these contacts than did the Canadian government, which was limited at that time to a few diplomats at Canadian posts in the capitals of Costa Rica, Guatemala, and Mexico, and had no permanent presence in either El Salvador or Honduras. Other nonsectarian associations loosely affiliated through the Canadian Council for Refugees similarly pleaded with the government to mount a larger-scale humanitarian effort for Central Americans in need.

An earlier chapter of this book discussed the expanded use of visas as a means of regulating would-be entrants to Canada. The issue of when to require visas from the nationals of a specific country is relevant to discussing Canada's decision to place Guatemalans in the designated class category in 1984, because the designated class measures were coupled with a visa requirement. This troubled Canadian immigration and refugee interest groups, who saw these government moves as further attempts to place orderly, managed entry above humanitarian considerations and safety for desperate people. The government's aim was to curtail and ultimately prevent the arrival at Canadian ports of entry of undocumented Guatemalans, and to carry out all necessary processing, including the issuing of visas, at immigration posts in Central America.

In the view of officials associated with the decisions both to add Guatamelans to the designated class category and to require entry visas of them, "Churches and advocacy groups such as Amnesty International are opposed in principle to the use of visas in this manner because, in their view, Canada should pursue an active first asylum policy. They mistrust the use of special programs to compensate, as they feel the selection involved may have an immigration bias."[26] Despite the disagreement of Canadian-based voluntary organizations and opposition members of Parliament, Guatemalans lost their visa-exempt status. Guatemalans seeking to enter Canada were processed abroad under the relaxed criteria of the designated class provisions in the immigration regulations. What this Guatemalan visa issue represented was a philosophical divergence between humanitarian organizations and liberal officials who advocated or at least supported a policy of Canada granting asylum, and the gatekeepers who preferred controlled, managed intake and resisted self-selection of entrants.

Violence and political unrest continued to be endemic in Central America throughout the 1980s, but were particularly intense during 1984. During that year John Roberts, the minister of employment and immigration, was informed by his officials that a growing number of Guatemalans who had not escaped from their country required urgent protection from officially condoned military death squads. This anxiety about the physical safety of people within Guatemala even extended to that of a few Canadian diplomats.[27] While not inclined to waive the newly authorized visa requirement, Canada, working closely with UNHCR representatives in the region, rapidly took steps to assist Guatemalans by completing their required documentation in the relative safety of nearby Costa Rica.[28]

A rather unusual feature of the Canadian assistance programs for Central American refugees involved official efforts to admit Central Americans who had already entered the United States illegally in search of safety and a better way of life. Washington's policy was to deport as many of these people to their countries of origin as quickly as possible. The illegals, primarily Salvadorans, had not been officially recognized by the American administration as bona fide refugees and were therefore constantly subject to removal. President Reagan's administration did not consider either El Salvador or Guatemala a refugee-producing state, although the human rights infractions in both these countries were well documented and deplored by many governments and humanitarian organizations. Often deportation would return these people to situations where they had a well-founded fear of persecution, a fundamental component of the 1951 Refugee Convention definition. The United States government's policy was tantamount to *refoulement*, which, as a signatory to the 1951 Convention, it had promised to avoid. With the knowledge of American authorities Canadian consulates in Dallas and Los Angeles, beginning in the early 1980s, issued entry visas to Central Americans threatened with deportation. Many American churches and liberal individuals associated with the sanctuary movement welcomed the

Canadian initiative and counselled persons in danger of deportation to avail themselves of the Canadian program.

Thousands of Central Americans remained in that part of the world and were in physical danger throughout the 1980s. It is somewhat surprising that during the mid-1980s, when the region seethed with violence, the numbers of people privately sponsored by Canadians under the provisions of the *Immigration Act* remained small compared with the Indo-Chinese movement.[29] As the decade closed, the level of violence declined noticeably but did not disappear. UNHCR officials noted, however, that substantial numbers of people who had been sheltered in holding camps in Honduras, Costa Rica, and Mexico, in some cases for years, began to return to their homelands.

REFUGEES FROM OTHER AREAS

While the three admissions programs discussed here constitute the most numerically significant ones mounted during the years the 1976 *Immigration Act* has been in force, they do not by any means represent Canada's entire effort to help refugees or people in refugee-like situations. Smaller groups of refugees and designated class members entering Canada have included Tamils from Sri Lanka, Christians from Lebanon, Iranians (primarily of the Baha'i faith), and Afghans.

Africa, the continent that according to UNHCR contains approximately half the world's refugees, has not been an important source for Canada's resettlement programs. To explain this the Canadian government has pointed to the official positions of both UNHCR and the Organization of African Unity (OAU). Both bodies have consistently asserted that when temporary or durable solutions to African refugee problems are being developed, emphasis should be placed on maintaining the people in question within Africa. Such a policy, they argue, encourages local integration of refugees into countries close to the refugee-producing state or states, and eventually repatriation. As a result, fewer than one thousand African refugees have entered Canada annually. Those who have entered have tended to be people from urban centres whose repatriation or successful local integration in nearby countries appears most unlikely because of their professions or past political activities.

In the view of senior officials involved in formulating Canada's refugee policy, it is probable that more attention will be paid during the 1990s to discovering and resettling African refugees who are in genuine danger. Moreover, as certain regions like Eastern Europe and Central America produce fewer refugees, Canada's selection and resettlement efforts will conceivably alter to include northeast and sub-Saharan Africa. As discussed earlier in this chapter, Canada has become increasingly concerned about ensuring that refugees receive protection from the international community and are not threatened with or subjected to *refoulement* or other human rights infractions. In the final decade of this century, UNHCR and the OAU appear to have taken less negative stands on refugee resettlement outside of Africa.[30]

Annually, as part of the report to Parliament on future immigration levels, officials reserve a few hundred places in the refugee intake projections for unanticipated refugee emergencies. These budgeted but unassigned positions are intended to enable Canada to respond quickly when unexpected refugee flows occur.

Canada's refugee and designated class resettlement programs have at least two broad goals. First, they are intended to alleviate the plight of some of the millions of distressed people. Second, it is hoped they will encourage other countries to do more to assist UNHCR and other international agencies cope with global refugee emergencies. Canadian refugee policy seeks to do more than resettle people who have fled their homelands in this country. Through financial contributions to refugee assistance agencies such as UNHCR, and diplomatic actions aimed at reducing the probability of new refugee-producing situations, Canada strives together with like-minded states to prevent unplanned and unwanted mass exoduses and to find durable solutions to those that have already occurred.

While government critics argue that Canada should adopt a more generous approach to refugee admissions, the programs themselves generally operate with little controversy and few administrative headaches. How to deal fairly and effectively with the thousands of people who arrive at Canadian ports of entry every year and claim to be refugees has proved to be a far more difficult political and managerial problem, and provides the focus of the following chapter.

7 Determining Refugee Status within Canada

Developing appropriate organizational and administrative procedures to ensure that the objectives of any public policy are met can be extremely difficult, no matter what the nature of the prevailing political system. In Canadian immigration policy, arriving at a satisfactory process for verifying refugee status claims by individuals already in Canada illustrates how taxing and frustrating it can be to try and marry policy goals with workable, yet just administrative measures. No other single aspect of policy during the life of the 1976 *Immigration Act* has produced as much contention and acrimony or required as much time and effort by officials and the responsible ministers. What is more, the protracted debate over how best to combine important administrative values such as fairness with efficiency in the refugee status determination process took place in a stressful policy environment, as more and more would-be immigrants, many ineligible for admission under prevailing regulations, saw this as a way into Canada.

Before the promulgation of the 1976 *Immigration Act* in 1978, no statutory reference concerning the issue of refugee status existed. For approximately five years preceding 1978, a committee of officials within CEIC had reviewed claims for refugee status from people already in Canada and passed on recommendations to the minister. The number of claims coming to the attention of that committee was insignificant compared with the thousands that required decisions annually by the mid-1980s. In 1976, for example, approximately 600 claims were made; 25 per cent were found to be valid, while an additional 15 per cent of claimants were permitted to remain in Canada for humanitarian and compassionate reasons.[1] Once the Canadian government had decided to recognize the international refugee phenomenon in law, the question remained as to how people already in Canada would have their claims for refugee status determined. While uncertainty prevailed about the appropriate mechanism, the minister, Robert Andras, and his political advisers and immigration officials knew exactly what they did not want. All were adamant that the responsible minister should not be directly involved in any way with status determination decisions. Ministers of immigration had been politically damaged too frequently in the past by appeals of all sorts directed to them. The *Immigration Act, 1976* therefore established a process that most officials considered both judicious and administratively manageable, with appropriate appeal procedures for claims ruled invalid. A few officials did express some misgivings about giving refugee status claimants universal access to the appeal process. These officials remembered only too well the early 1970s when, as described in chapter 5, an enormous backlog at the Immigration Appeals Board resulted finally in the suspension of Regulation 34, which had permitted potential immigrants to apply for landed immigrant status from within Canada. This prescient anxiety, however, did not carry the day.

THE FIRST STATUS DETERMINATION
PROCESS AND ITS PROBLEMS

The *Immigration Act* called for the creation of the Refugee Status Advisory Committee (RSAC), which would be responsible for deciding the validity of claims and thereby ensuring that people would not be arbitrarily deported to states where their lives or freedom would be endangered. The Committee included immigration officials, private citizens appointed by the minister, and an official from DEA. In addition the representative in Canada of the UNHCR had the right to attend RSAC sessions to ensure that Canada adhered to its obligations under the 1951 Refugee Convention. RSAC's authority did not extend to people claiming refugee status at immigration posts outside Canada. Evaluating such claims remained the responsibility solely of visa officials at those posts. The provisions for determining refugee status from within Canada represented a cautious but noticeable liberalization of government attitudes, in keeping with the overall thrust of the 1976 Act.

The refugee status determination process contained several stages. The Act and subsequent regulations required the applicant to make the claim to an inquiry officer during a removal hearing or, if the applicant was in status, to approach an official at an inland Immigration Centre. (The term "in status" is used to describe an individual who is in Canada legally, e.g., a visitor or a student.) An official took the claimant's statement under oath and forwarded this transcript to RSAC. If RSAC found the claim to be valid, the applicant would be notified in writing but had to await the completion of medical and security checks before landed immigrant status was offered. If RSAC's decision was negative, the claimant could appeal to the Immigration Appeals Board (IAB) for redetermination, at which time the written transcript would be reviewed. Should the Appeals Board's decision also be negative, the claimant could take the case still further, to the Federal Court, but only on points of law or interpretation.[2]

From the outset critics expressed unhappiness with this process. These observers, familiar with the global refugee phenomenon, had some doubts about the fairness and justice of the status determination system. The inability of the claimant to appear in person before RSAC for an oral hearing constituted one of the strongest grievances. Opponents of the process argued that a written transcript, the basis on which the judgment was to be made, could not provide a comprehensive, foolproof means of determining the merit of a claim: they pointed out that RSAC had no opportunity to ask questions of the applicant or observe his or her demeanour and behaviour.

This complaint invariably brought the following response from immigration officials, even before the machinery had been set in place. "The proposal that all claimants have a right to appear personally before the RSAC may be desirable in principle. Unfortunately, it would create totally unacceptable delays and defeat the objective of this Department."[3] In another effort to justify opposition to claimants appearing in person before RSAC, a senior official wrote: "The suggestion that all claimants should have the right to a full hearing is apparently motivated by a genuine concern that is, moreover, one which on the surface at least, would seem to be supported by common sense. In fact, it is a suggestion which if put into effect, would create very real difficulties because to the extent we allow personal access to the RSAC and the Immigration Appeals Board, we expose the system to the danger of being overwhelmed by non bona fide claimants, clogged by delay and obstructed by legal entanglements."[4]

It appears that the officials who drafted the refugee status determination provisions of the 1976 Act did not anticipate large numbers availing themselves of the machinery. Certainly, they did not expect the process to become a routine channel for evading the normal admission requirements and getting easy access to Canada. Most officials assumed RSAC was available to identify possibly a few hundred people annually who would be seeking refugee status to avoid removal to a state where their freedom or lives might be threatened.

The issue of oral hearings for claimants remained a major concern throughout the first half of the 1980s, and was inextricably connected in the minds of officials with the need to avoid creating a backlog of refugee claimants. Small pilot projects were undertaken in Toronto and Montreal during 1983 that allowed claimants whose requests had been rejected by RSAC to appear in person before an IAB panel for redetermination of their status. If the oral hearing process could be added without significantly contributing to the dreaded backlog, opposition among immigration officials was expected to diminish. Critics of the refugee status determination process welcomed the pilot oral hearings but they were not expanded and, in fact, were discontinued within months, probably because of the extended time they required.[5] To institutionalize oral hearings before the IAB for refugee status redetermination, the prevailing legislation had to be amended.

Whenever any amendments to the *Immigration Act* were contemplated, senior officials and the minister's political advisers became increasingly anxious that parliamentary and voluntary sector critics would take the opportunity to launch a wide-ranging attack on policy generally. It is almost a given that the highly emotional character of immigration issues causes the government of the day to present legislation to Parliament only when no other alternative is possible. Even with this well-known axiom in mind, immigration officials recommended that the minister inform the House of Commons Standing Committee on Labour, Employment and Immigration that legislative changes permitting oral hearings before the IAB would soon be at the drafting stage. Prior to tabling any new legislation in Parliament, however, practical politics dictated that other troublesome aspects of refugee status determination policy should also receive attention so that a whole package of related legislative modifications could be brought forward simultaneously.

Since 1981 ministers of employment and immigration had established special task forces and hired outside consultants in an effort to discover how, when dealing with refugee status claimants, they could meld justice and fairness with the seemingly incompatible goals of administrative efficiency and control. The changes that had resulted from these earlier studies tended to be rather superficial, representing little more than tinkering; they certainly were not of the scope needed to streamline the status determination procedures. The most significant move yet taken in what was to be a long list of attempts came in the spring of 1984 with the appointment by John Roberts, then minister of employment and immigration, of Rabbi Gunther Plaut. Rabbi Plaut was requested to develop alternative models that would ensure fairness and also eliminate the backlog of claimants that was becoming worrisome to the authorities.[6] More than a year passed before the Plaut Report was completed and released by the government.

When Canada's overseas refugee selection operations were discusses in the previous chapter, it was pointed out that NGOs, led by the churches and Amnesty International, were very active and not without influence. This was even more the case when it came to criticizing the government's refugee status determination procedures. Informed officials somewhat reluctantly acknowledged that these organizations assisted immigration settlement programs in helping refugees and their dependants adjust to life in Canada. One senior Immigration NHQ official described church-based groups, for example, as "representing a cross section of refugee workers without whose voluntary activities it would be difficult to deliver our refugee resettlement program."[7] The major Canadian churches, coalescing under the national umbrella of the Inter-Church Committee on Refugees, felt especially strongly about the need for oral hearings. Meeting the requests of this body would smooth relations with an organization whose efforts in the area of refugee relief were considerable. Furthermore, CEIC officials preferred to deal with well-informed, realistic national voluntary bodies rather than with locally based groups, whose idealism and inexperience could hamper good relations between the government and the voluntary sector. This is not to suggest by any means that the leading refugee advocacy groups in Canada and the immigration bureaucracy shared a common outlook. In fact, the opposite was true when deliberations over a revised refugee status determination process were taking place.

In general terms, immigration officials and the activist NGOs addressed the whole refugee policy area from quite different perspectives. Church-based bodies as well as Amnesty International saw the plight of millions of distressed people as requiring government-to-government and person-to-person assistance. They had little patience with legalistic, rigid refugee definitions. The situation was described to the then minister of employment and immigration, Flora Mac-Donald, by her officials as follows: "To these NGOs, there is no question of making distinctions between individuals from countries in turmoil on the basis of their circumstances and needs. It is rather a situation of responding to requests for assistance based on the Judeo-Christian ethic that to give succour to the homeless is a responsibility whatever the motive behind the individual's request."[8] Yet in the minds of much of the immigration bureaucracy, if everyone making a request were considered to be a refugee, few if any would be protected. The memo concluded, "We cannot expect to blunt their criticism through one single response or a range of responses as are available to us within the current legislative framework because there is nothing we can do to satisfy their collective aspirations."[9]

The long, rancorous debate over oral hearings came to an abrupt close in the spring of 1985 when, in a landmark decision, *Singh v. Canada (Minister of Employment and Immigration),* the Supreme Court of Canada ruled that claimants had a right to appear personally before a panel of the Immigration Appeals Board in cases of refugee status redetermination. The battle for the right to oral hearings, at least for appeals, had been won. As a result of this judgment, the government introduced amendments to the Immigration Act in Parliament in June 1985, authorizing the IAB to expand to up to fifty members from the original eighteen. This proposed expansion reflected the prevailing view among Immigration NHQ personnel that universal oral hearings would add substantially to the time required to handle status redetermination cases before the IAB, and that it was imperative to prevent an increase in the backlog of claimants.

The proposed amendments failed to receive quick passage through the House of Commons. As many officials and the minister's political advisers had anticipated, the debate over the amendments was seen by members of Parliament as well as refugee advocacy groups as a rare but ideal opportunity for an extensive attack on government policy. Opposition MPs and activist NGOs asserted that, by expanding the IAB, the government was pre-empting its promised consideration of modifications to the refugee status determination process, about which Rabbi Plaut had prepared his report and recommendations. The government, for its part, argued that passage of the amendments would not result in other options being dismissed. Passage would at least enable the status redetermination process, which was already overwhelmed, to continue until new machinery could be agreed on. The legislation necessary to increase the size of the IAB was finally approved by Parliament in early March 1986, allowing a full complement of board members to be in place by autumn. While it was hoped that the issue of oral hearings had at last been put to rest, the solution had only served to exacerbate the backlog.

Although few officials had thought in the late 1970s that the numbers of refugee status claimants would clog the determination system, no other part of the entire immigration field caused so much difficulty for officials and their ministers. No single situation accounted for the backlog, but contributing factors included global migratory pressures, the impatience of would-be immigrants or their Canadian sponsors with normal immigration selection procedures, and long-term government indecisiveness about how best to repair the inadequate process.

It did not take officials long after the promulgation of the *Immigration Act* in 1978 to recognize a noticeable increase in the queue of refugee status claimants. Any backlog of refugee claimants could, in fact, serve as an incentive to people who were not refugees but who wanted access to Canada to use the status determination channel. By late 1978 one official observed, "We must move quickly to streamline the system to ensure that rapid processing time will benefit serious claimants while discouraging abuse."[10] From the outset of the refugee status determination process, all agreed that the system must remain credible. The following decade would see the government modify the original status process in an effort to aid genuine refugee claimants while discouraging frivolous applications, and thereby regain the system's credibility.

During the first year or two that the RSAC functioned, the growing backlog was partly a result of the committee's mode of operation. In the first half of 1979 the RSAC heard an average of eight cases weekly. Estimates indicated that RSAC members spent between seven and ten hours reading the necessary documentation on each case.[11] Efforts to help members digest the documentation more expediously were made, and additional members were named to the committee so as to establish more panels. These comparatively minor changes failed, however, to keep up with the mounting number of claimants, many of whom by 1980 were illegal economic migrants reaching out for this final means of avoiding removal from Canada.[12]

By the early 1980s pressure had mounted within and beyond the government for the adoption of more humane yet efficient procedures for the settling of refugee status claims. In certain cases, the media publicized the circumstances confronting claimants, embarrassing the immigration bureaucracy and its minister. The Task Force on Immigration Practices and Procedures, established by the minister, Lloyd Axworthy, reporting on immigration policy issues in 1981, pinpointed the problem: "The serious consequences and high public profile of many refugee claims dictate that particular care be given to the selection of the procedures which are established for dealing with them."[13] The report continued: "The best way of avoiding the dangers of appearing arbitrary and unfair is to ensure that our refugee determination procedures reflect Canadian standards of procedural fairness as they have become manifest in our general concept of a fair hearing."[14] The report perceptively pointed out that administrative convenience, a desire for efficiency, and a wish to impose vigorous control were not always compatible with justice and compassion. The conclusions of the task force proved to be more liberal than the views held by many control-oriented immigration officials at NHQ. The report, for example, asserted that officials should not assume claimants were prone to abuse the system. Anxiety over fraudulent claims, it continued, should not erase impartiality and the sense of justice required to maintain fairness.[15]

One symbolic but significant step taken during 1982 to create a sense of distance between the enforcement-minded philosophy of some NHQ officials and the RSAC was to relocate the committee in premises separate from the immigration program and to have its chair appointed from outside the ranks of immigration officials. To emphasize the separation from the operational side of NHQ, the RSAC chairman then reported to the minister or the minister's delegate, rather than to a career official.

With the backlog of refugee status claimants growing constantly, immigration officials renewed their drive for a broader use of the visa requirement to prevent undocumented arrivals at Canadian ports of entry immediately posing as refugees and joining the queue for a hearing. The prevailing view among policy makers at immigration NHQ was that requiring visas would prevent unprocessed migrants boarding aircraft at distant departure points and then entering the refugee claimant queues in Canada. As discussed elsewhere in this volume, DEA officials opposed the indiscriminate broadening of the visa requirement for foreign policy reasons. DEA also pointed out that extending the use of visas would require additional personnel at overseas posts, something for which it had no resources from Treasury Board.

Near the end of 1983 the backlog had grown to the extent that to clear it, using the existing status determination procedures and assuming no new claimants joining the queue, would have taken up to three years.[16] Scaling down their requests for extensive additional visa requirements, immigration officials proposed that such documents should at least be mandatory for nationals from states with consistently high levels of refugee claimants, such as Guyana, Sri Lanka, and Guatemala. DEA did ultimately agree to this more moderate approach.

In addition to a somewhat greater use of the visa mechanism, immigration officials in cooperation with DEA adopted other tactics aimed at slowing the flow of would-be refugees. Canadian authorities sought to identify ports of departure abroad from which large numbers of claimants had begun their journeys to Canada. These facilities were monitored more closely to catch potential abusers at their points of origin. In addition airlines were made financially responsible for the cost of detaining undocumented persons reaching Canadian airports. This became a highly contentious issue between the Canadian government and the airlines, as more and more migrants, intending to claim refugee status in order to remain in Canada, destroyed their documents while on board the aircraft. Canadian officials went so far as to suggest that the airline cabin crews should collect and hold passengers' documents until the aircraft reached Canadian ports of entry, but this was rejected by the air carriers. These and other proposals from immigration officials reflected the desperate attempts being made to stem the flow of aliens who inevitably expanded the backlog of refugee status claimants.

Despite minor adjustments in the refugee status determination process and attempts to detect new fraudulent claimants and prevent them from joining the ever-growing queue, the backlog mounted. By 1984 it was abundantly apparent to all that only through substantial legislative changes might the problem be alleviated. But what this legislation should contain, or for that matter what procedures should be adopted to determine that content, gave rise to vociferous debate within CEIC and beyond. The problem confronting the government was really twofold: how to develop a refugee status determination process that would in the long term prevent a backlog and, in the interim, how to deal with the existing queue. The apparent need to have the status determination process universally available lay at the root of the matter. Having the system open to anyone without any preliminary screening appealed to civil libertarians and refugee assistance groups but daunted many immigration officials at NHQ and at Canadian ports of entry. The problem was identified clearly in a memorandum prepared by a senior official during 1985. "It is evident that the very existence of such a universal mechanism can act as a magnet for persons seeking admittance to Canada. This leads to exponential increases in the caseload faced by the status determining body and ultimately results in the collapse of the system and the desire for a general amnesty."[17]

What proved to be an important ingredient in the search for a solution came in the spring of 1985, with the tabling in Parliament of the report commissioned a year earlier from Rabbi Gunther Plaut by John Roberts, the minister of employment and immigration. The report, entitled *Refugee Status Determination in Canada: Proposals for a New System*, constituted the most comprehensive investigation of the issue to date. It was also the first and only occasion on which the minister had looked to an entirely independent source for a solution to the refugee status determination imbroglio. Rabbi Plaut stated in his report that as a signatory to the 1951 Convention Relating to the Status of Refugees, Canada was obliged to give protection to persons found to be refugees and not return them to where they might be endangered. Canada's humanitarian tradition, in his view, added a moral imperative to this legal requirement. Officials responsible for meeting and dealing with refugee claimants must be humane and sensitive to their plight and should recognize how they differed from routine immigrants. His introductory section concluded with the assertion that whatever structure and procedures were ultimately decided on for determining refugee status, they had to be entirely independent of political influence.

After commenting critically on the existing refugee status determination system, Rabbi Plaut proposed a comprehensive new approach emphasizing principles of natural justice and fairness, yet also embodying procedures for deciding the validity of claims expeditiously. Succinctly put, Rabbi Plaut's scheme called for a "Refugee Officer," a new position filled by people sensitized to the psychological and physical terror confronted by genuine refugees, to meet with the claimant within twenty-four hours of the request being registered. This official, adopting a nonadversarial manner, would interview the claimant with a panel of the proposed Refugee Board being present. A decision would be taken promptly and, if it was negative, the claimant could appeal to the Federal Court. In the report, Rabbi Plaut set out in considerable detail how the Refugee Board would function and what the prevailing structure would look like. The report concluded by reiterating that the process for hearing and deciding on claims for refugee status had to operate in such a way as to assure the Canadian public that bona fide refugees would receive permission to remain. The process had to be seen to be just and capable of making judgments within a short time.[18]

When examining the recommendations for a new system, whether from the Plaut Report or from other in-house task force reports, the government sought to ensure that the modified procedures would be able to withstand court challenges and would not soon need to be altered again. To assess the reaction of informed refugee assistance and advocacy groups to the Plaut recommendations, CEIC held a series of public consultation sessions throughout the summer and early autumn of 1985. By means of the consultation process, CEIC tried to maintain a dialogue with some of its critics while not committing itself to any specific proposals. If the informed voluntary associations supported a particular process for refugee status determination, the chances of a court challenge would, of course, be lessened.

The firmly held views of some refugee advocacy groups, determined to win generous treatment for claimants, helped to polarize the government, particularly immigration policy makers, and these organizations. Influential immigration officials at NHQ believed that these somewhat more radical voluntary associations wanted a process that would replace immigration control with a multitude of protective measures for claimants. This NHQ school of thought regarded the number of fraudulent claimants as so serious that every effort had to be made to deter them, while still not preventing genuine refugees from having their status recognized. According to this view, public sympathy for refugees could only be maintained through effective regulation of the determination process, which would improve its credibility. In spring 1987 proponents of this outlook recommended that the moderate refugee assistance groups persuade their more outspoken associates to tone down their criticisms of the minister. "The responsible proponents on the non-governmental side must also realize there are practical limits and unless they publically support her [the minister's] approach, and openly tell their more radical elements to face reality in the matter, the result could be a very restrictive system."[19]

While CEIC weighed the merits of various legislative modifications during 1985 and 1986, the existing refugee status determination process continued to operate, albeit inadequately. In these years statistics indicated that the percentage of claimants acquiring refugee status through the system varied from 91 per cent and 66 per cent for those from Somalia and Iran respectively to zero for those from Lebanon and Pakistan.[20]

During the early and mid-1980s, increasing numbers of claimants faced serious financial problems while awaiting either their initial hearing before the RSAC or, if it rendered a negative decision, the subsequent appeal. Claimants were not eligible for employment authorizations and, therefore, could not seek work legally. As a result, many claimants and their dependants became destitute and ended up on provincial or municipal welfare rolls. Others, of course, chose to work illegally or had financial support from relatives and friends already in Canada. Provincial and municipal governments, believing these people were Ottawa's responsibility, urged the federal authorities to grant refugee claimants employment authorizations until final decisions on their status had been made. Officials at CEIC, already alarmed by the lack of effective deterrents to claiming refugee status, rejected these appeals. Permission to work would, in their view, simply encourage more people to make refugee claims. This issue, especially important in Ontario and Quebec where the majority of claimants had temporarily settled, remained unresolved until new legislation regulating the refugee status determination process became law in 1989.

The process of deciding on a new, efficient yet fair system for determining refugee status within Canada took place in several fora. Within CEIC, the Refugee Affairs Division and the Immigration Practices and Procedures Task Force had grappled with the issue in the early 1980s. Later two experts, Professor Edward Ratushny of the Faculty of Law at the University of Ottawa and Rabbi Gunther Plaut, had each been commissioned to prepare separate reports with recommendations. During 1985 the minister had established another task force, headed by an experienced senior immigration officer and including other proven officials from various units at NHQ. Its objective was to examine the reports and recommendations already completed and to draft legislation that would once and for all make the refugee status determination process workable while satisfying critics. As this newest task force deliberated, the flow of refugee claimants into Canada became a flood. Even with Immigration Appeals Board membership expanded from eighteen to fifty during 1986, the number of appeals from negative RSAC decisions heard by the panels that year barely surpassed 3,000. Meanwhile, 18,000 new claims were made during 1986; in 1987 the number reached 25,000.

Blatant fraudulence could be easily detected among a growing proportion of these claimants. The approximately 4,000 Portuguese and 2,000 Turkish nationals who requested refugee status during 1985 and 1986 fell into this category. So too did the 800 Brazilians who made similar claims during the initial two months of 1987. Despite the frivolous nature of these claims, those making them were still entitled to use the status determination system and did so in an attempt to prolong their stay in Canada. By far the most dramatic event of this period was the discovery of 153 Tamils in small boats off the coast of Newfoundland during the summer of 1986, which caused public anxiety and made the entire immigration and refugee policy areas appear to be out of control. All these circumstances increased the momentum of the development of new legislation.

Exacerbating the backlog still more during the mid-1980s, a growing number of people claiming refugee status arrived in Canada through border crossings from the United States. Changes in American immigration policy accounted in large part for this increase. As of November 1986, modified American regulations granted an amnesty to people who had been in the United States illegally before 1982. The other side of the coin, of course, was that individuals who had entered the United States illegally since that year were subject to deportation. Thus many illegal aliens, a high proportion from turbulent Central America, looked to Canada as a potential haven. In February 1987 the Canadian government took steps to discourage the entry of these and other aliens assumed to be potential refugee status claimants. The most significant changes to Canadian regulations and procedures included the following. First, the list of eighteen countries previously considered definite refugee-producing states, and whose nationals had automatically received minister's permits when arriving in Canada, was cancelled. Second, people entering Canada from the United States and claiming refugee status would now be required to remain on the American side of the border until an immigration hearing could take place. Third, people passing through Canada from states from which visitor visas were required would now have to acquire transit visas. Finally, provisions of the special programs for the nationals of Iran, Lebanon, Sri Lanka, El Salvador, and Guatemala were modified in an effort to discourage people from these countries with relatives already in Canada from arriving before the completion of appropriate processing abroad.[21]

The policy changes preventing refugee claimants from the United States entering Canada before a hearing gave rise to substantial criticism from the usual Canadian interest and advocacy groups. These organizations believed that requiring refugee claimants to wait in the United States placed these people in danger of deportation by American authorities, although the Canadian government considered this most unlikely.

NEW LEGISLATION AND A NEW PROCESS

Measures such as those adopted in February 1987 still did not constitute the major changes that were needed to erase the backlog of claimants and prevent a new one from forming. The alterations did, however, signal the probable introduction of substantially more restrictive legislation intended to curtail abuses to the system.

By May 1987, when a portion of the promised major legislation received first reading in the House of Commons, the backlog of refugee status claimants stood at nearly 50,000. The new legislation, Bill C-55, had taken years to formulate and draft. Bill C-55 was intended to protect genuine refugees in need, process claims fairly and quickly, curb abuses, and manage resources effectively. The proposed legislation established a three-stage process for verifying claims for refugee status at Canadian ports of entry or at inland immigration offices.

The legislation set forth the following procedures. First, immediately after notifying officials of the intention to make a claim, an applicant was to be heard by two persons, an adjudicator who was an immigration officer trained for this task, and a member of the Convention Refugee Division of the newly created Immigration and Refugee Board (IRB). This initial stage determined whether the applicant was eligible to proceed to the second stage, where the credibility of the claim was at issue. The applicant went to the second stage unless both the adjudicator and the IRB member cast negative votes. To be eligible to proceed to stage two, the claimant must not already have had refugee status or something similar to it granted in a third country, and must not have had a serious criminal record. At the second stage the claimant had an oral hearing before a two-person panel composed of members of the Convention Refugee Division of the IRB. This stage, where the authenticity of the claim was assessed, had a nonadversarial format and, according to Bill C-55, would occur within days of stage one. Both members of the panel had to cast negative votes to prevent refugee status from being awarded to the claimant. Should the panel reject the claim, the applicant could be granted leave to appeal the decision on points of law to the Federal Court, the third and final stage of the process. The legislation called for the claimant to await the ruling of the Federal Court in a "safe country," but the claimant would be returned to Canada at the government's expense if the court decided in his or her favour.

The arrival of 174 Sikhs from India on the shores of Nova Scotia in July 1987, less than a year after 153 Tamils from Sri Lanka had been found in small boats off Newfoundland, added to the public's anxiety over the rise of uncontrolled migrants and provided the government with justification for a second piece of refugee policy legislation. Like the Tamils, the Sikhs had paid an unscrupulous ship's captain to take them from a Western European port to Canada, where they intended to seek refugee status even though many were primarily economic migrants. Those who were genuine refugees had already been granted, or were eligible to be considered for, refugee status in the countries of Western Europe from which they had sailed. During the remainder of 1987 and into the following year, rumours persisted that other boats carrying undocumented migrants could be expected to reach Canada.

In August 1987 Parliament was hurriedly recalled for a special session at which Bill C-84 was introduced. The intent of this legislation was to deter and punish unscrupulous people who profited from counselling and assisting undocumented migrants to come to Canada and knowingly make fraudulent refugee claims so as to circumvent prevailing immigration regulations. Bill C-84 sought to prevent abuse of the immigration system by imposing harsh penalties on convicted smugglers and their accomplices and severe fines on transportation companies bringing people without the necessary documentation to Canada, and by detaining people who arrived in Canada without having been processed abroad.

Both Bill C-55 and Bill C-84 met with considerable opposition within and beyond Parliament. Literally dozens of different criticisms were voiced by concerned refugee assistance and advocacy groups and opposition MPs. The two principal criticisms of Bill C-55 were the following: First, claimants had no guarantee of a hearing before a panel of the IRB at stage one, where the eligibility screening occurred. Second, the concept of a "safe country" where claimants were to await the results of their appeals seemed vague and undefinable. Anxiety over the content of Bill C-84 was equally widespread and intense. The critics primarily attacked provisions that enabled Canadian authorities to turn back ships suspected of carrying illegal migrants while they were still at sea. This would, in the minds of many observers of international refugee phenomena, constitute *refoulement*, which Canada, as a signatory to the 1951 Refugee Convention, had undertaken to avoid. Bill C-84 also permitted undocumented migrants claiming refugee status to be held in detention for up to twenty-eight days without a hearing, which critics asserted contravened the *Canadian Charter of Rights and Freedoms*. Refugee assistance groups disagreed strongly with those provisions of Bill C-84 that could be used to imprison church-based and other refugee advocacy workers for counselling potential claimants on how best to acquire refugee status.

The government defended both pieces of legislation aggressively, arguing that backlogs composed of fraudulent refugee claimants could only be avoided by reducing the number of steps in the determination process and removing any incentives for making false claims. Canada, through these two bills, hoped to emulate the policies of other First World states that were also trying to restrain uncontrolled movements of undocumented migrants, especially from the economically less developed parts of the world. By severely tightening up the refugee status determination process, the two bills would keep Canada in step with Western European governments and the United States as global migratory pressures mounted at the ports of entry of most First World countries. The legislation and its accompanying regulations represented a victory for those segments of the immigration bureaucracy and the federal cabinet that saw management and control as being pre-eminent in preserving the integrity of the immigration system.[22]

Both bills encountered strenuous examination in the House of Commons during the late summer and autumn of 1987. Although the opposition, urged on by articulate supporters from the voluntary sector, argued for modifications to remove the most controversial aspects of the legislation, the government's large majority easily allowed the bills to pass virtually unchanged. The then Liberal-controlled Senate, however, failed to give prompt assent to the legislation; in fact it demanded a series of alterations earlier rejected by the government when the bills were before the House of Commons. Bills C-84 and C-55 were returned to the lower House in late 1987 with at least a dozen proposed amendments. Barbara McDougall, the minister of employment and immigration, was still unprepared to accept most of the suggested changes, but, under mounting pressure from the opposition and concerned refugee assistance groups, the section permitting the turning away of ships from Canadian ports was dropped. That provision of Bill C-84 had reminded too many people of the fate of the St. Louis, a ship which, in 1939, had been chartered by German Jews in search of sanctuary but had not been permitted to land passengers at any ports.

Intermittently during the winter and spring of 1988 the two bills continued to be the objects of acrimonious debate inside and outside Parliament. The rhetoric from their opponents reached new heights, asserting that the legislation was contrary to natural justice, human rights, and civil liberties. The government, for its part, held to its long-standing position that to prevent abuses to the refugee status determination system, rigorous action in the form of firm legislation was essential. Ultimately the weight of the government's majority in the House of Commons, plus the growing attacks on the upper House, an unelected chamber, for holding up passage of other legislation (including the Canada–United States Free Trade Agreement), prevailed. Both Bills C-55 and C-84 received the Senate's reluctant approval in July 1988, and royal assent within days.

During the extensive time that elapsed before Bills C-55 and C-84 were passed into law, immigration officials at NHQ continued their efforts to cope with the seemingly endless backlog of refugee claimants and began planning the implementation of the new legislation. Despite the best attempts of the RSAC and the enlarged IAB, the backlog at the start of 1988 included 4,000 more claimants than it had a year earlier.[23] This was attributable to a 1987 decision of the Federal Court. The government had made it known that only some of the members of the IAB would become members of the IRB when that body came into existence with the passage of Bill C-55. It was clear that the government's attitude towards fraudulent refugee claims and undocumented migrants had hardened significantly since the unexpected arrival of the Sikhs and Tamils. Some IAB members may have concluded that their chances for appointment to the new IRB would be enhanced if they made negative rulings on cases forwarded to them for redetermination. The Federal Court, therefore, ruled that there was a possibility of bias when the IAB heard appeals from negative RSAC decisions.[24] As a result, virtually no appeals from negative RSAC decisions were heard by the IAB during the last few months of its life.

Developing training manuals for bureaucrats responsible for administering the new legislation as well as for the members of the new IRB placed additional demands on the already heavily occupied officials at immigration NHQ. Recognizing the need for additional personnel, Treasury Board awarded the Immigration Program at CEIC more than 200 additional person years for the 1988–89 fiscal year, largely to meet the expected start-up requirements and to assist in clearing up the backlog of refugee status claimants.[25]

With rumours rampant in the country and abroad of more boat-loads of undocumented migrants trying to reach Canada's shores, officials developed elaborate contingency plans. The supposed would-be refugees, according to sources in Western Europe, might be expected to reach Canada's Atlantic coast during the summer or autumn of 1988. Steps were taken to locate facilities in which to detain hundreds of illegal entrants, whether they arrived by sea or by air. Proposed locations in Ontario and Quebec, the provinces expected to receive most of the undocumented arrivals, included under-used Canadian Forces bases. No refugee claimants, however, arrived by boat as the Tamils and Sikhs had in 1986 and 1987. At the same time, expecting that Bills C-55 and C-84 would soon become law, officials proceeded to put in place machinery capable of removing up to 1,000 rejected refugee claimants per month, and to delineate responsibility at NHQ and in the field for operating this and other programs arising from the new legislation.

Other officials at CEIC and DEA began generating a list of the "safe countries" provided for in Bill C-55, where rejected claimants would await decisions on their appeals. From the earliest debates over Bill C-55, the "safe country" concept had been one of the most abhorrent features of the legislation to opposition MPs and refugee assistance organizations. Concerned Canadians viewed the prospect of "safe countries" with alarm for a number of reasons, of which three stand out. First, criteria for a "safe country" had not been spelled out to the satisfaction of the concept's opponents. A so-called safe country might not deport all the claimants awaiting a Canadian decision to their original homelands, but a certain number of selective removals might occur. Second, what appeared to be a "safe country" one week might, as circumstances changed, subsequently become quite dangerous for the nationals of certain countries. Would Canadian officials be able to monitor global conditions closely enough to ensure that people awaiting the results of their appeals would not be removed by the government of a "safe country"? Finally, in the minds of critics, and possibly even some officials, it was anything but certain that foreign governments would willingly accept, even temporarily, people awaiting the results of their appeals from the Canadian refugee status determination process. That Canadian authorities might, in fact, consider the United States a "safe country" particularly troubled church-based refugee workers and Amnesty International. As discussed in the previous chapter, the American government during the 1980s had routinely removed nationals of El Salvador and Guatemala to their homelands, where many observers believed they faced death or at least imprisonment. At the same time, concerned Canadians recognized that it would be extremely difficult politically for Canada not to include the United States, that self-proclaimed bastion of liberty, in any list of "safe countries." On 28 December 1988, just days before Bills C-55 and C-84 were to come into force, the Canadian government announced that the "safe country" provisions of the legislation would not be implemented for the time being. It is by no means certain why the government chose to delay implementing this feature at the last moment. Possibly the arguments set out above had convinced Barbara McDougall, then the responsible minister, and her political advisers.

On 1 January 1989 the new process for verifying refugee status claims became operational. The primary mechanism in this process is the IRB, the largest Canadian administrative tribunal. This board consists of two sections, an Immigration Appeals Division similar to the former IAB and a Convention Refugee Determination Division substantially different from its predecessor, the RSAC. The board's headquarters are in Ottawa, with branches in Montreal, Toronto, Winnipeg, and Vancouver. The chair of the IRB is appointed for a seven-year term and is the equivalent of a chief executive officer in a private corporation. The chair reports to Parliament through the minister of employment and immigration. Each of the board's two divisions has a deputy and an assistant deputy chair. The Convention Refugee Division may have up to sixty-five full time members, a minimum of 10 per cent of whom must be lawyers. The remainder are drawn from a broad spectrum of Canadian society. The IRB's members have a comprehensive support structure to draw on, including a refugee documentation library responsible for monitoring events around the world that could produce or have produced refugees.[26]

During the initial year that the IRB functioned, refugee advocacy groups, immigration lawyers, opposition members of the House of Commons Standing Committee on Labour, Employment and Immigration, and the media watched intently for a breakdown in the new system and the appearance of another backlog of claimants. For the year ending 31 December 1989, 21,745 claims were made by people entering Canada and seeking refugee status, while the IRB rendered 6,268 decisions. The rate of acceptance for cases heard in 1989 was 76 per cent, considerably higher than the RSAC rate, which had averaged approximately 25 per cent during the committee's life.[27]

During the IRB's first two years it attracted outspoken criticism from the usual sources regarding its ability to cope with new claims for refugee status. Many well-informed observers asserted that the new structure would be overwhelmed and flounder under the stress of any sizeable influx of claimants. To the surprise of these critics, the fears they had expressed appear to have been unfounded, or at least exaggerated. Writing in a publication of the UNHCR, a Canadian journalist, author of a long list of articles often critical of government refugee policy, stated, "Many people now feel that Canada's asylum process has achieved a high degree of credibility."[28] The manifestly unfounded claims have been generally driven off. For the 1990–91 fiscal year, the IRB received a budget increase of approximately 20 per cent from the Treasury Board. In late 1990 92 per cent of those entering the process were found eligible to pass to the second stage where the authenticity of claims is assessed. Finally, the productivity of the IRB's panels appears substantially higher than that of the old RSAC panels. Nevertheless, a certain number of modifications continued to be needed to prevent the recurrence of an unmanageable backlog of claimants.

The creation of the new refugee status determination process in 1989 still left the Canadian government with an enormous problem: the backlog of claimants that had been expanding since the mid-1980s. At the close of 1988 the backlog stood at 122,000 cases, a number far too great to be handled by the new untried determination process. The government decided on an administrative review of each claim, and promised that this could be accomplished within a two-year period. The habitual critics of refugee policy remained justifiably skeptical. Clearing the backlog actually required over three years.

As this and the preceding chapter have demonstrated, formulating and implementing a refugee policy has proved an extremely difficult task for both Liberal and Conservative governments. Politically oppressed or economically deprived people determined to escape from danger and hardships will continue to migrate to more desirable locations and will use whatever means necessary to do so. The pressures on Canada to admit more and more migrants will continue. The government hopes that the number of undocumented arrivals at Canada's ports of entry can be severely reduced, forcing people to revert to Canada's preferred course of action, processing at immigration posts abroad. Whether this will occur, of course, depends a great deal on how efficient processing is at these overseas offices, as well as at inland immigration centres in Canada.

8 Federal-Provincial Relations in Immigration

Any requirement that two jurisdictions share legislative and administrative authority over a policy field can result in added complexity at best and policy paralysis at worst. In Canada, immigration and agriculture are the two policy areas over which, since Confederation, Ottawa and the provinces have had concurrent constitutional authority. It is the premise of this chapter that the extent to which provinces become involved in the formulation and administration of immigration programs can be measured, in large part, by a form of cost-benefit analysis. In other words, provincial governments have been and continue to be content to leave the federal government dominant in immigration except when they perceive Ottawa's actual or proposed actions to be economically harmful or, in the case of Quebec, culturally damaging.

As discussed in chapter 2, determining and dominating immigration policy, as Ottawa has for much of Canada's history, has provided few if any political benefits for the federal government. Given this reality, provincial governments see little advantage in entering fully into immigration policy unless, by their own efforts, they can acquire benefits otherwise unlikely to accrue to them, or protect interests they perceive to be endangered. This chapter identifies those aspects of immigration, such as entrepreneurial and investor immigration and settlement services, which have comparatively recently motivated a certain level of provincial activity.

Under section 95 of the *British North America Act, 1867*, now the *Constitution Act, 1867*, legislative authority over immigration is a concurrent power. During Canada's first century, however, the provinces demonstrated only sporadic interest in it, preferring to leave this often politically troublesome and sensitive field to Ottawa. By remaining comparatively aloof from immigration matters, provincial politicians were free to take advantage of whatever few political benefits could come their way in a policy area that seldom brought much public approbation to the federal government.[1]

During the 1960s, this provincial inaction began to break down as Ontario, British Columbia, and especially Quebec, the provinces receiving by far the most immigrants annually, sought a role for themselves. Quebec established a full-fledged department responsible for culture and immigration while the other leading receiving provinces adopted a variety of approaches and programs, chiefly designed to supplement existing federal and nongovernmental settlement schemes for immigrants. By the late 1980s provincial interest in immigration policy and related regulatory issues had expanded significantly to include business immigrants, labour and manpower planning, international child adoption, and an extensive range of settlement services.

The federal government has shown a certain ambivalence in the face of this mounting provincial involvement in immigration matters. The prospect of sharing with provincial governments some of the growing expenses associated with elaborate settlement programs for newcomers appears attractive. However the provinces, initially through the Meech Lake discussions and more so since the accord's rejection, have given notice that the collaboration in their view involves a good deal more than simply picking up some of the settlement costs. Thus the sharing of authority has not been confined to expenditures on settlement programs but has seen the provinces, again Quebec especially, insist on playing a role in selecting the type and number of immigrants and managing and determining the content of settlement programs. Provincial entry into the core areas of immigration activity has eroded but not as yet ended the traditional federal dominance in this field. The rejection of the Meech Lake Accord added fuel to the already noticeable efforts of major receiving provinces to gain greater influence over immigration, and negotiations since the demise of the accord indicate that provincial participation in immigration will become much more extensive.

FORMAL AGREEMENTS WITH THE PROVINCES

Sections 7 and 109 of the *Immigration Act, 1976* provide the statutory explanation for the comparatively recent prominence of the provinces in immigration affairs. The Act requires the federal government to consult with the provinces during the annual process of estimating the immigration intake for the subsequent year. Ottawa and the provinces are also, under the provisions of the Act, encouraged to negotiate and sign agreements ensuring the involvement of both levels of government in the annual immigration levels determination exercise. The circle of officials responsible for drafting the Act during the mid-1970s gave considerable thought to how explicitly the provinces should be brought into the immigration policy-making process. Most provinces had not demanded a voice but Quebec had and this, possibly more than anything else, indicated to the federal politicians and bureaucrats drafting the new legislation that statutory recognition of a provincial role was required.

Possible changes to increase the provincial role considered at the time of the Act's drafting included sharing authority over setting the weights in the point system, providing for provincial immigrant sponsorship, and establishing joint federal-provincial selection mechanisms for immigrants, to the extent of having officials from both government levels work together as teams at overseas visa posts.[2] Quebec and Ottawa successfully negotiated a comprehensive agreement which, among other points, contained this last option. Otherwise, the federal efforts came to be focused on reaching umbrella agreements with the provinces to fulfil the statutory requirement for consultation. The agreements Ottawa envisioned called for a minimal apparatus consisting of committees of provincial officials who would advise the federal minister responsible for immigration on the number of immigrants each province deemed appropriate for resettlement annually. In addition, each committee would try to harmonize economic, demographic, and social aspects and establish priorities through consultation.[3] As of 1991 seven provinces had joint agreements with Ottawa, the majority having been negotiated and implemented during the first years the 1976 Act was in force. The most elaborate were the agreements between Ottawa and Quebec, which are examined later in this chapter.

The agreements with provinces other than Quebec are very similar, reflecting the federal government's aim of arriving at a common framework for collaboration that would suit the needs and interests of all the provinces except Quebec. In practice the existence of formal immigration agreements has not made much difference to the interaction between the two levels of government. Provincial efforts when dealing with federal authorities have focused on designating occupations for which a domestic labour shortage exists, developing settlement services, and encouraging business immigration, especially under the entrepreneurial and investor programs.

While the federal cabinet and its advisers in the Privy Council and Prime Minister's Offices may have favoured the provinces becoming more active in immigration, this sentiment was less in evidence among senior members of the immigration bureaucracy at NHQ. These officials, already well aware of how complex and time-consuming it was to manage the recruitment and selection of immigrants, recognized only too well the impact additional provincial involvement would have on the process. One memorandum, written in 1987 shortly after the Meech Lake Accord had been drafted by the prime minister and the ten premiers, asserted that if other provinces wished to negotiate constitutional agreements on immigration similar to the one then being discussed with Quebec, "the situation would become untenable. It would be virtually impossible for the federal government to demonstrate leadership and exercise its responsibility for the national standards and objectives of immigration policy."[4]

SETTLEMENT SERVICES

While the provinces may be tempted to enlarge their activities in the immigration field, fiscal realities are likely to act as a brake. It seems improbable that any of the provinces except Quebec will seek a role in overseas recruitment and selection of immigrants except in the area of business immigration. Yet reception and adaptation programs, which operate within the province and are highly visible, may attract more attention from that jurisdiction. Federal officials, when contemplating any expanded role for the provinces in settlement programs, point to the question of how to maintain equal access to services. As in other policy fields when the issue of consistent national standards is debated, aspirations to an ideal solution may give way to considerations of financial and political feasibility.

The Canadian government, urged on by ethnic and other organizations in the voluntary sector as well as by the provinces, has recognized that an immigration policy entails more than simply selecting people who wish to establish themselves in the country. Incrementally to be sure, Ottawa, recently joined by some provinces, has achieved a policy that promotes the integration and adjustment of newly arrived immigrants to their frequently unfamiliar surroundings. This acceptance of the need to assist immigrants to become acclimatised has only been evident since midcentury. Previously, what assistance immigrants did receive tended to be offered by family, friends, and members of their own ethnic group through churches and fraternal organizations. Throughout most of Canada's first century, most immigrants received no government support while trying to establish themselves, surviving in large part due to their tenaciousness. In the minds of many Canadians, including politicians and public servants, how quickly and successfully an immigrant and that immigrant's dependants adapted to life in Canada said much about the inner strength and character of these newcomers. While by mid-century the federal government operated a substantial set of social programs such as unemployment insurance and old age pensions, these were not particularly directed at immigrants. Throughout the 1950s and 1960s, the amount of federal or provincial funds devoted to immigrant adjustment and adaptation remained comparatively small.

Settlement services received attention in the 1976 *Immigration Act*. Section 3(*d*) states that one of the goals of immigration policy is "to encourage and facilitate the adaptation of persons who have been granted admission as permanent residents ... by promoting cooperation between the Government of Canada and other levels of government and non-governmental agencies in Canada." While this subsection of the Act avoids any explicit mention of funding, in practice federal financial support for language and job training, counselling, and similar services has been available. The premise underlying federal efforts in the settlement services field is that immigrants and their dependants who receive adequate social support, economic assistance, and offers of advice at the outset will more quickly become productive and well-integrated members of Canadian society. Funds may have to be expended to achieve this, but in the final analysis this investment will be repaid to the state time and time again by the newcomers through taxes, job creation, and simply by their being law-abiding citizens. Thus settlement programs have two objectives: first, to give immigrants personal confidence and competence in adapting to life in Canada, and second, to provide Canada with new residents who can contribute to the overall strength and diversity of the country.

Although some segments of society may continue to believe that government support for immigrants is unnecessary, or even demeaning to the able-bodied, experienced immigrant assistance agencies in the voluntary sector as well as knowledgeable federal and provincial officials wholeheartedly endorse the concept of settlement programs for newcomers. Authorities today acknowledge that their responsibility does not end with the arrival of the immigrant at a Canadian port of entry. It is in the public interest to maintain a support network for immigrants, at least during the initial stages of their adjustment.

At the federal government level, at least three departments play a role in the settlement field. Health and Welfare, the department least involved, funds medical support schemes, particularly for refugees and members of designated classes, who are covered for up to one year or until they are eligible for provincial health care programs. CEIC and the Department of the Secretary of State have much more significant involvements with the settlement field. For some years, in fact, a certain amount of confusion has existed in the voluntary sector about how jurisdiction for settlement services is divided between these two departments. In general, officials in the Department of the Secretary of State formulate and administer programs with long-term impact on immigrants, such as those concerned with multicultural-ism. During the life of the present *Immigration Act*, CEIC has acquired the broadest mandate in the settlement field. Its settlement services focus on receiving immigrants at ports of entry, assisting them in finding employment, funding language training programs and, depending on the newcomers' circumstances, helping them with accommodation and other daily necessities. CEIC officials at district offices may also offer counselling to newly arrived immigrants and inform them of the wide range of provincial, municipal, and volun-tary services available to them. If the newcomer is a privately spon-sored refugee, CEIC acts as a facilitator, bringing the two parties together and subsequently offering support when needed. In many instances, CEIC does not offer all of these services directly, but rather contracts with voluntary organizations on a fee-for-service basis.

The Immigration Program within CEIC funds and directs settle-ment services through two major schemes, the Immigrant Settlement Adaptation Program (ISAP) and the Adjustment Assistance Program (AAP). ISAP operates primarily through community based nongov-ernmental organizations across Canada, providing funds for the ser-vices indicated above. By the mid-1980s, more than 130 locally based voluntary associations had contractual arrangements with Ottawa to provide adaptation help to newly arrived immigrants.[5] Immigration officials believe the voluntary sector can provide these valuable ser-vices both more effectively and at less cost than CEIC could itself.[6] By the mid-1980s an estimated 75,000 people annually were receiving some form of adaptation support from contracting organizations, at a cost to CEIC of approximately $2,200,000.[7] By 1990 the budget allocation for ISAP had reached $7,000,000.[8]

For its part, AAP provides support for people who are considered virtually destitute. Newcomers eligible for AAP, primarily govern-ment-sponsored Convention refugees and members of designated classes, have their daily subsistence requirements for such items as housing, food, and clothing met for up to one year following their arrival in Canada. For such people, AAP constitutes the safety net necessary to their successful adaptation and integration. AAP also makes substantial demands on the federal treasury; it cost almost $70,000,000 annually by the close of the 1980s.[9] Through contracting voluntary organizations immigrants to Ontario receive close to 40 per cent of ISAP and AAP funds, while those in Quebec and British Columbia regularly collect the next largest portions. As of April 1991 Quebec has assumed responsibility for its settlement services, although the province continues to receive some transfer payments from Ottawa for them.

Services offered directly or funded by the Settlement Branch at CEIC operate on the premise that recipients see Canada as their new, permanent place of residence. Visitors, foreign students, and temporary workers are ineligible for these services. Settlement services operated or funded by Ottawa are monitored and regularly evaluated as part of an ongoing assessment process. Relations between the Settlement Branch at CEIC and the numerous contracting voluntary agencies have generally been cordial and businesslike. To be sure, from time to time the smaller, understaffed agencies have found the extensive paperwork associated with receiving federal funds time consuming and irritating. These same agencies also complained periodically about the lapse of time between submitting the required forms and payment by the Settlement Branch. These annoyances did not derive from any fundamental flaws in the overall process and, for the most part, have been overcome.

For most of the period the 1976 *Immigration Act* has been in force, the federal government's approach to immigrants has stressed that people entering the labour market should receive the greatest amount of assistance. This has been particularly apparent with respect to language training and counselling services. Women, students, and the growing number of immigrants classified as entrepreneurs and investors have generally not received as many of these mainstream services. As the 1990s began this practice came under increasing scrutiny and has, in fact, been altered to attempt a more equitable distribution of services among all newcomers. Such a policy decision represents more than a cosmetic change and has led to an altered set of priorities in the dispersal of settlement services. The alteration came about after the government realized that integration programs needed to be substantially improved. Having announced its intention to accept up to 250,000 immigrants and refugees annually by 1992, Ottawa acknowledged that increased efforts had to be made to help all categories of newcomers adapt to their new land. CEIC aims "to provide a policy framework to guide settlement and integration programs across federal departments; insure greater collaboration with the provinces, private sector and non-governmental organizations in the delivery of settlement and integration services; set new directions in language training and increase funding to make a more flexible range of options accessible to a greater number of immigrants; and to place more importance on understanding the values of immigrants and they ours."[10]

Settlement services, no matter which level of government provides them, have not received anything like the attention paid to refugee status claimants or business immigrants by the public or media. This lack of interest in the settlement field is not the result of the excellence or even adequacy of such programs. Moreover, the quality of life in Canada can be affected by the extent to which immigrants have been satisfactorily integrated into the social milieu. Social tranquillity in an ethnically diverse community is more likely when adjustment services are properly publicized and easily accessible to immigrants.

Ontario, the initial destination of at least 40 per cent of immigrants, is one of three provinces that have no written agreement with Ottawa on immigration matters. Yet, without any formal bilateral arrangement, the government of Ontario and federal settlement authorities based at CEIC's regional offices in Toronto are routinely in contact about program delivery. This ad hoc approach has always been the Ontario government's preferred form of managing immigration settlement issues. Provincial officials do have a more specific role to play with Ottawa when it comes to selecting and monitoring business immigrants.[11]

In January 1991 Ontario's minister of citizenship indicated that the province was considering various options that would result in Queen's Park having more to say about immigration issues. In particular, Ontario sought more influence over immigrants likely to find their way into the labour market. Ontario had previously steered clear of any formal arrangement that would have it playing any role in the recruitment and selection of immigrants. It is probable that some institutionalized process for jointly selecting immigrants will be negotiated between Ontario and Ottawa.

BUSINESS IMMIGRATION

While family reunification remains the cornerstone of Canadian immigration policy, providing economic benefits for all regions of the country through immigration remains a high priority as well. Labour market requirements have been a major determinant of the direction and content of immigration policy throughout Canada's history. A less-known aspect of this part of immigration policy stems from the desire of Ottawa and the provinces to recruit individuals with entrepreneurial spirit and the capital necessary to establish new businesses and create jobs. Businessmen prepared to take risks with their investments have always been welcomed and, in the past decade, have been courted energetically by provincial and federal officials. Business immigration programs have, like most other segments of immigration policy, required consultation and cooperation both between relevant federal departments and between Ottawa and the provinces. Recent programs in this area have met with mixed reactions from informed sectors of Canadian society.

The entry of immigrants with capital and managerial skills is as old as Canada itself. No special attention was paid to this class of newcomer, however, until the 1950s and 1960s, and even then what interest there was seemed largely confined to providing occasional settlement services. The truth was that by the late 1970s, without real planning or effort by any level of government, people with capital were arriving in the country eager to purchase or found enterprises. As one official wrote, "Think what we could do if effort were put into it."[12] Officials did, in fact, begin at about that time to put some thought into attracting people with capital who were either self-employed or could provide employment opportunities for individuals already in Canada. During 1977 a special unit was established at immigration NHQ to develop an active yet selective entrepreneurial program that would encourage foreign businesspeople to consider immigrating to Canada.[13] From the outset CEIC placed as much emphasis on managerial experience and the likelihood of job creation as on the amount of capital possessed by the prospective newcomer. Investing in real estate, for example, was a goal common to many potential immigrants with capital, but to Ottawa and the provinces such proposals, which did nothing to create jobs or additional goods, proved unattractive.

By the late 1970s the provinces had clearly made their own keen interest in business immigration known to federal authorities. Under the consultation provisions of the *Immigration Act, 1976*, discussed in chapter 4, CEIC had responsibility for dealing with the provinces on questions relating to the type and number of immigrants to be admitted annually. Just how large a part the provinces should play in recruiting business immigrants and evaluating their entrepreneurial proposals remained uncertain at the time. CEIC did not want to make the consultation process unnecessarily detailed, but it was well aware that overseas visa officers did not have the competence to assess the merits of business propositions.

During the first half of the 1980s, Canada's business immigration program was directed at individuals in two categories, self-employed and entrepreneur. Both were included in the independent class, one of the four groups which, along with the family, refugee, and designated classes, made up the classes admissible for permanent residence. The self-employed classification applied to individuals who frequently came from the professions and the arts. While these self-employed people would not hire anyone, they did bring skill and talent with them and were considered desirable immigrants. The entrepreneur classification applied to people arriving with at least a quarter of a million dollars to invest in an existing or new enterprise that they would manage and which would create or maintain employment for one or more Canadians.[14] Applicants in this class were required to have a business proposal evaluated initially by the overseas visa officer and then by the province in which the business was to be established.

In January 1986 the government altered the immigration regulations in order to establish an additional category within business immigration, the investor class. This category marked a refinement of, rather than a major change in, the direction of the business immigration program. The investor category was intended for people who had considerable capital to invest in a Canadian enterprise but were not interested in the hands-on management of it. As with the entrepreneurial class, the goal remained to create or maintain jobs. Investors were not required to participate actively in the operation or management of the enterprise. Their funds, rather than any managerial skill or talent, would gain entry to Canada for them and their dependants. The investor scheme was built on the belief that this approach would help to fulfil the overall objectives of business immigration policy: to promote, encourage, and facilitate the immigration to Canada of experienced businesspeople with risk capital.

Those falling into the investor category of business immigration had three options to choose from. They could place funds in a new, approved commercial or business venture, a privately administered investment syndicate, or a government administered venture capital fund.[15] According to a senior CEIC official, "the underlying principle of the investor category is not only the continued emphasis upon the applicant's skills and qualifications as a successful businessperson, but also as well that person's willingness to take risks by linking his/her investments to needed job creating enterprises which contribute to business development."[16]

Despite some criticism, discussed below, Canada's business immigration program has operated comparatively successfully over the past decade. Overseas visa officers, with the enthusiastic support of provincial authorities, have tapped a pool of entrepreneurs and investors eager to try their hand in Canada. The smaller and less affluent provinces, often bypassed by immigrants flowing to large urban centres, have become some of the keenest advocates of business immigration. Admittedly these provinces have attracted only a small proportion of the incoming capital and management skills, but they otherwise might not have acquired even these.

As strongly as business immigration has been endorsed by the provinces, support for it was even greater among CEIC officials and Progressive Conservative MPS during the years their party was in power. Early in the Mulroney government's first term in office, the phrase "Canada is again open for business" exemplified the outlook of many cabinet ministers and back-benchers alike. Dismantling the Foreign Investment Review Agency and replacing it with Investment Canada represented one dimension of this philosophical approach. Programs aimed at attracting entrepreneurs and investors also appealed to like-minded bureaucratic policy makers.

Ministers responsible for immigration and their political advisers during the Mulroney government, together with their provincial counterparts, were positively effusive about the success of all aspects of business immigration. Statistics indicate that the number of jobs created or maintained and the capital invested in enterprises have been substantial. Yet the total numbers arriving in this category have not significantly cut into the flow of those entering in the other admissible classes.[17] Hong Kong remains the chief source for entrepreneur and investor immigrants, but arrivals from Lebanon and Iran have not been inconsequential. Canada's banking and financial sector strongly endorsed business immigration. Programs that aim to create jobs and bring new capital mesh well with the objectives of major actors in the private sector. These newcomers who can inject additional managerial talent and funds into the business community are seen as natural allies by the already established corporate community.

Despite broadly based government and corporate support, business immigration programs have not been without their critics. Yet no strong coalition of opponents has confronted policy makers. Philosophically, a comparatively small percentage of Canadians object to schemes that encourage the settlement in Canada of capitalists and promoters, pursuing goals these critics see as inimical to the public interest. People holding these views tend to be on the radical fringes of organized labour and, while vocal, are numerically insignificant. Added to these critics are a few small businessmen already operating Canadian enterprises who feel somewhat vulnerable and potentially threatened by the arrival of newcomers with large amounts of capital who are capable of becoming commercial rivals. Screening of entrepreneurial and investor applicants by provincial officials is intended to minimize this anxiety.

Other critics are not so much opposed to the premises behind business immigration as convinced that officials spend a disproportionate amount of time and effort attempting to attract entrepreneurs and investors, at the expense of family and refugee class candidates. It is difficult to evaluate the validity of this sort of observation. Provinces such as British Columbia that are anxious to attract business immigrants argue, to the contrary, that visa officials have not expended enough time and effort on these schemes.[18]

A further criticism, again more philosophical than pragmatic, has arisen as a corollary to the long-standing "brain drain" issue. Some Canadians with a genuine concern for the fate of the world's less developed states charge that business immigration schemes lure already scarce managerial and entrepreneurial talent away from capital-deprived countries. Defending the programs against such criticisms, CEIC officials contend that immigration schemes should not purposely set out to discourage or prevent qualified and eligible people from emigrating. Proponents of business immigration point out that many Third World countries have rigid restrictions on the exodus of capital, to avert exactly what these opponents of the business programs fear would occur. Informed observers acknowledge that entrepreneurs and investors will search out business opportunities wherever they may be. If Canada failed to establish programs to attract these people, Australia and the United States, among other possible destinations, would be more than happy to welcome this type of immigrant.

The sort of criticisms of business immigration programs described here reflect, for the most part, the views of special and minority interests. There is little if any evidence to suggest that opposition to the objectives of business immigration has been widespread. With this form of immigration, as with immigration programs generally, public dissatisfaction has arisen from perceived program abuse. Bogus business proposals from unscrupulous entrepreneurs and investors have damaged the credibility of business immigration schemes. When the rules are adhered to, Canadians accept the value of new managerial talent and investment capital. When foreign business owners, operating with the advice of unscrupulous consultants or lawyers, establish dummy enterprises and fraudulent residences in Canada and generally fail to fulfil the requirements of the programs, the public understandably becomes impatient and outspoken.

At the time of writing, with Canada in an economic recession, any public irritation with business immigration has diminished. It has been replaced with at least tacit support for policies trying to attract people with managerial capabilities and capital who promise to maintain or create jobs.

QUEBEC'S INVOLVEMENT IN IMMIGRATION

Earlier in this chapter I stated that, of all the provinces, Quebec has been the most deeply involved in immigration affairs. A number of factors account for this. First, Quebec's place in Canada as a result of language and culture is unique. In an era when millions of words have been spoken or published on this subject, the statement is at least a given, if not a cliché. Second, beginning with the Quiet Revolution of the 1960s, Quebec has striven to exercise authority over all fields in which it has constitutional jurisdiction. Immigration, as a concurrent power shared by Ottawa and the provinces, fell into this category. Third, as Quebec's birth rate declined, influential segments of the province's society urged Quebec City to do everything possible to increase the flow of immigrants who either spoke or were prepared to learn French. During the 1960s the Quebec government indicated a desire to participate with Ottawa in recruiting and selecting immigrants, rather than confining its activities to settlement and adjustment services, the tendency of other provinces. By the close of that decade Quebec had established its own Department of Culture and Immigration and was making efforts to attract more newcomers, who were seen as essential if this community of French-speaking people was to survive in North America.

The federal government did not attempt to obstruct Quebec's growing interest in immigration. Instead, it moved cautiously so as to appear sensitive to Quebec's goals and to demonstrate its willingness to negotiate formal arrangements. In 1978 the two governments signed the Cullen-Couture Agreement, named after the ministers responsible at the time for immigration in the two jurisdictions. Although Ottawa had entered into vague, unspecific umbrella arrangements with several other provinces during the late 1970s, the Cullen-Couture Agreement was an explicitly operational undertaking by both parties. Among the items in the agreement were procedures whereby Quebec and Ottawa jointly selected immigrants at overseas visa posts. Quebec also acquired the authority to choose people in the independent class and shared responsibility with Ottawa for the allocation of points in the selected worker programs when such individuals were destined for that province. In the settlement field, the Quebec government developed more of its own capabilities in adaptation and adjustment services, leaving less to the voluntary sector. The agreement, according to CEIC's deputy minister, "is recognized as a positive example of how the federal government can work jointly with the Province of Quebec with a spirit of shared understanding and cooperation."[19] Through the Cullen-Couture Agreement Quebec had become a partner, and a dominant partner in the settlement area, with the federal government.

Relations between federal and Quebec officials and ministers responsible for immigration have not been without irritants, but they have not been especially tense or acrimonious either. Officials at CEIC's NHQ acknowledged in 1985 that the Cullen-Couture Agreement was cumbersome and restricted the federal government's ability to pursue national policies and standards.[20] Some of the operational and administrative problems arose from differing methods of dealing with sponsors and applicants rather than from any real philosophical divergence. Both governments over the years recognized the benefits of the arrangements, which could be attributed to the effectiveness of the Cullen-Couture Agreement and of a successor plan that came into force in April 1991.

Throughout the thirteen years that the Cullen-Couture Agreement was in use, immigration issues relevant to Ottawa and Quebec were supervised and administered by two joint committees. One, co-chaired by CEIC's executive director of immigration and Quebec's deputy minister of culture and immigration, addressed policy matters with a view to coordinating the approach of the two jurisdictions. The second committee, comprising middle-level officials from both governments, dealt with operational and procedural matters. The first committee met infrequently, while the second proved to be more active as it coped with day-to-day functional problems.

Even though the Meech Lake Constitutional Accord failed to be ratified within the required three-year period, some of its provisions, such as those referring to expanded immigration powers for the provinces, remained very much alive. In December 1990 the federal and Quebec governments announced the successful negotiation of a new immigration agreement, based on the principles set down earlier in the Cullen-Couture Agreement, to come into force on 1 April 1991. The press release announcing the agreement indicated that its primary thrust was the provision of settlement services, which would now fall exclusively within the purview of the province of Quebec. According to the press release, "The agreement, subject to the Canadian and Quebec Charters of Rights, respects the mobility rights of immigrants as well as their right to protection against all discrimination ... It acknowledges that Canada has exclusive responsibility for setting national standards and objectives [while] Quebec has exclusive responsibility for the selection of immigrants in the independent class and assigns to the provincial government responsibility for reception, linguistic, cultural and integration services as well as economic integration services."[21] The arrangement resulted in Ottawa withdrawing entirely from these services and providing financial compensation to Quebec so that the services it offered would be "equivalent overall to those services offered by the federal government elsewhere in Canada."[22]

In this closing decade of the twentieth century, the provinces have entered the immigration field to a degree never seen before. They perceive some aspects of immigration to be very much in their own interests and intend to adopt policies and programs that stand to benefit them. Not surprisingly, the major receiving provinces have more at stake and are, therefore, developing what they see as appropriate measures. While Quebec has specific objectives in the immigration field that set it apart from the other provinces, all of them are attracted by the potential economic gains offered by various forms of business immigration. At the same time, the provinces, led by Quebec, are demonstrating a heretofore uncharacteristic willingness to play an ever increasing role in offering settlement services.

Canada appears to be entering a period of unprecedented decentralization of federalism. In many instances provincial governments are no longer satisfied merely to consult with Ottawa on immigration or, for that matter, any policy issue. They want to possess either exclusive power or at least dominant authority over a growing list of areas, including immigration. Provincial governments are no longer prepared to depend on Ottawa to identify or defend their interests. It is to be expected, therefore, that provinces other than Quebec will enter into discussions with Ottawa aimed at reaching agreements not unlike that achieved by Quebec in 1991.

9 Linking Immigration and Demography

In chapter 4, the annual consultation process leading to the setting of immigration intake levels was discussed. As indicated there, considerations such as family reunification, humanitarian principles, compassion, and the economy's ability to absorb skilled and unskilled labour are among the factors that determine the annual target figures. An additional ingredient not examined in that earlier chapter, which over the years oscillates in importance among policy makers' priorities, is demography. Since the mid-1980s the question of an optimal size for Canada's population and how that population should be distributed in terms of age has again risen on the government's list of policy priorities.

Throughout virtually all of Canada's history politicians, business leaders, journalists, and a host of other would-be experts have made unsystematic, impressionistic assertions about the desirable size and composition of Canada's population. In the post–World War II years, or even earlier for that matter, magazines and newspapers frequently carried articles addressing the issue that their authors referred to as Canada's absorptive capacity. Politicians' speeches and journalists' articles dwelt on Canada's comparative emptiness, the need for an adequate but not excessive supply of labour, and a desire for immigrants prepared to live on what even as late as the 1940s was still perceived as potentially desirable agricultural land. The hope of enticing immigrants to settle in places other than rapidly growing urban centres, preferably on the land, has been a persistent factor in much of the deliberations of parliamentarians and journalists well beyond the mid-twentieth century.

Interest in determining an optimal population size for Canada diminished substantially during the 1950s and 1960s, pushed aside partly by unprecedented economic growth and partly by a birth rate that, at the height of the "baby boom," approximated three children for every woman of child-bearing age.[1] By the 1970s a number of factors had converged to stimulate a more systematic and sustained interest in Canada's optimal population size.[2] Among these were an increased Canadian awareness of rapid global population growth, a multilateral effort to analyse the impact of that growth at the United Nations–sponsored Bucharest Conference in 1974, the publication by CEIC of the *Report of the Canadian Immigration and Population Study* as a forerunner of a new *Immigration Act*, and an emerging interest in population issues in Canada on the part of a small but active group of academic demographers.

The basic "givens" that form the starting point for any demographic analysis of a state's present or future population are neither esoteric nor especially complex. There are four fundamental variables that are ultimately responsible for the size and rate of population growth: fertility, mortality, emigration, and immigration. While government policies and services can have a limited effect on the first three of these variables, the one most routinely regulated in a liberal-democratic society is the fourth. Taxation laws or other incentives may have some impact on birth rates but, generally speaking, the number of children a woman chooses to have remains a very personal decision. Mortality rates can also be somewhat affected by the extent of the public health and medical care available in a state but, like taxes, death is inevitable. Tampering in any way with an individual's ability to emigrate is unacceptable in a pluralist, liberal society. Thus immigration remains the population determinant most permissibly open to government regulation.

Numerous reasons exist for why a society may consciously endeavour to shape its own size, age distribution, geographic settlement patterns, and population density. As examples, the cost per capita of public services, the availability of job opportunities, the size and composition of the domestic market for goods and services, and the overall tax base for providing government with revenue are all significantly affected by demography. Similarly, a society with an expanding aging population will need to spend public funds on more medical care and housing for the elderly. Dozens of other implications of demographic factors could be cited. The significance of and need for a Canadian population policy gradually became apparent to immigration officials and some parliamentarians as the *Immigration Act, 1976* was being drafted and debated.

EARLY INTEREST IN A POPULATION
POLICY

As discussed elsewhere in this study, sections 7 and 109 of the *Immigration Act* require Ottawa to consult with the provinces when arriving at the annual immigration intake projections. Federal ministers responsible for immigration during the 1970s strove to convince the provinces to sign formal agreements with Ottawa as a means of ensuring effective, ongoing consultation on immigration and population issues. Some officials and informed observers believed that the rising need for a population policy would be the issue enticing the provinces into this new area of federal-provincial relations. To the surprise and disappointment of Robert Andras, the minister responsible for immigration during the years in question, only Quebec and Alberta showed any real interest in demographic issues and, in Alberta's case, that interest did not convert into any immediate willingness to sign a formal agreement with Ottawa.[3] Federal officials had expected that joint advisory committees with each province would assist policy makers in harmonizing economic, social, and demographic aspects of immigration. Quebec, as the preceding chapter explains, had a keen interest in virtually all immigration and demographic issues and eagerly sought entry into this policy field so long dominated by the federal government.

Within Immigration NHQ, some officials, junior and middle-ranking personnel for the most part, attempted in the late 1970s to establish a demographic unit. Although it received lip-service in reports and some publications, the attempt failed at that time, due in no small part to the lack of support from most senior officials at CEIC and to ministerial ambivalence, particularly in the Cabinet Committee on Social Policy.[4]

In the late 1970s and the early 1980s immigration officials did try to weigh demographic factors to some extent when processing applicants at overseas posts, but their efforts were not especially successful. As family class applicants received the highest priority in processing by law, and as their numbers continued to be large, officials simply had less opportunity to select people from the independent class who might have provided the diversity necessary to satisfy demographic considerations. With Canada's low birth rate and a noticeably aging population, demographic principles called for increased numbers of young immigrants who already had, or potentially would soon have, progeny. To produce a certain mix in the immigration flow would have required additional processing personnel, at additional expense. The absorption of the Immigration

Program's Foreign Branch by the Department of External Affairs in 1981 (discussed in chapter 11) added to the complexity of managing the immigration process and diminished the likelihood of demographic considerations receiving attention. Immigration reports, press releases, and projections generated at Immigration NHQ routinely referred to demographic factors as major components in determining the nature of the annual immigration intake. Yet, for administrative, financial, and political reasons, immigration officials did not pursue demographic goals very strenuously. With the benefit of hindsight, demographic objectives in immigrant selection can be seen to have been almost irrelevant in practice; certainly they remained unfulfilled.

GOVERNMENT ACTIVITY: THE HEALTH
AND WELFARE REVIEW

With the end of the economic recession of the early 1980s and the election of the Mulroney government in 1984, CEIC officials within the Immigration Program appear to have made renewed efforts to address issues of long-term significance in immigration and demography. Among officials knowledgeable about demographic principles, the prevailing attitude was to try at least to maintain population stability until the government of the day demonstrated the political will to formulate achievable elements of a population policy for Canada. Indications of this long awaited crystallization of political will were noticeable less than a year into the Mulroney government's first term. After considerable preparatory work, a document entitled *Report to Parliament on the Review of Future Directions for Immigration Levels* was tabled in June 1985. The report presented an overview of the relationship between demography and immigration policy and explained why a general review of immigration trends and requirements was in order. There was some question at the outset whether CEIC would be the department directing what could become the first step toward formulating a population policy, or whether such a task would fall more appropriately to another federal entity. Even the officials at Immigration NHQ most professionally interested in demographic aspects of immigration recognized that research leading to a credible population policy for Canada should involve many more considerations than immigration alone. It had even been suggested that an interdepartmental committee might be a convenient method of coordinating the population policy review.[5]

The immediate message of the June 1985 report to Parliament was that the government, even before proceeding to formulate a full-fledged population policy, had decided on a course of action that would promote "moderate and controlled growth in immigration."[6] It seems probable that demographic factors accounted to a substantial degree for this "controlled growth" decision. By the 1980s, for example, the Canadian birth rate had fallen to 1.7 children per woman of child-bearing age, well below the 2.1 needed for replacement. Moreover, projections indicated that over 20 per cent of the Canadian population would be sixty-five years of age or older by the early years of the twenty-first century, meaning younger people would be needed to fill jobs and to pay into the private and public social insurance programs.[7]

The June 1985 report also cleared away the mystery of where the responsibility for the demographic review would be centred. Jake Epp, then the minister of health and welfare and chair of the Cabinet Committee on Social Policy, had an interest in demographic and population issues dating back to the mid-1970s, when he had served on the special joint committee whose report and recommendations had provided the basis of the 1976 *Immigration Act*. Although CEIC had an administrative unit described as the Migration and Demographic Directorate, Flora MacDonald, the minister of employment and immigration, appears to have welcomed Jake Epp's interest in demographic and population matters. Since immigration officials could be seen as having a vested interest in the sort of demographic review undertaken, having it directed by another department would remove any sense of a conflict of interest. Jake Epp, then, would be the person responsible for the overall study during the subsequent three years. An assistant deputy minister in the Department of Health and Welfare, Dr. Michael Murphy, himself a demographer, would have "hands on" direction of the work. As Health and Welfare had no in-house demographic capability, plans called for specific studies to be commissioned from the academic community.[8]

Interest in demographic issues was also apparent elsewhere during 1985. In the spring of that year the very active House of Commons Standing Committee on Labour, Employment and Immigration had tabled the second of what would ultimately total nine reports on aspects of immigration. This particular report focused on potential demographic priorities and economic considerations. Under the rules of the House of Commons, the government was required to respond to standing committee reports and recommendations within 120 days of their being tabled; to a large extent, the June 1985 report to Parliament mentioned above constituted this reply.

The standing committee had argued for a Canadian population of 30 million by the close of the century, asserting as well that efforts needed to be made to lower the average age of the population. The government's response was generally noncommittal, urging patience until the recently announced demographic review could be completed.

During the summer of 1985 the Canadian Employment and Immigration Advisory Council (CEIAC) published its own report containing comments on a range of population and immigration issues. This advisory council, composed of individuals appointed by the minister and concerned with employment and immigration issues, had been established at the time the 1976 *Immigration Act* was proclaimed, to provide independent views for the minister. Like the report of the standing committee, the CEIAC study also focused on such factors as the falling birth rate and how immigration could be a positive force, filling a perceived need to prevent any increase in the proportion of the Canadian population that would be at or approaching the age of retirement by the century's close.[9]

Also during 1985 Flora MacDonald, the minister of employment and immigration, made renewed attempts to involve the provinces more meaningfully in the consultation process, particularly in the area of future population goals. In a letter to provincial governments, the federal minister elaborated on Ottawa's position that immigration must not be allowed to decline but rather should be considered as an asset contributing to Canada's growth in the future.[10] This and other correspondence indicates that the federal government was quite prepared to take the lead in pressing for moderate, controlled growth through an active immigration program, but was eager to have explicit provincial concurrence.

Unquestionably, the centrepiece among all these efforts to promote renewed interest in population questions remained the three-year demographic review directed by Health and Welfare Canada. Immigration officials at NHQ acquiesced in its sister department being assigned the lead responsibility for the study because Health and Welfare had experience in a number of matters central to population policy such as aging, pensions, and the increasingly skewed population mix. According to Jake Epp, the responsible minister, the goals of the demographic review were "to evaluate, extend and integrate the empirical evidence for relationships between demographic and other social and economic variables in order to contribute to the review of specific social and economic issues by the government and general public."[11]

Health and Welfare Canada endeavoured to present the demographic review as something quite out of the ordinary. It was to be much more than any routine internal exercise and would have a strong academic and scientific component, with peer review of commissioned projects. The review was envisaged by Dr. Murphy, its director, and his associates as a broadly based activity aimed at providing policy makers and other interested observers with the data necessary to arrive at informed decisions on population policy. Dr. Murphy and his colleagues did not envisage concrete policy recommendations being contained in the review. The government's decision to embark on this review was welcomed by academic demographers as well as by informed individuals and groups long interested in population issues.

Among those officials in the Immigration Program at CEIC interested in demography and the application of the review's content to policy, initial optimism was gradually replaced by mounting anxiety. Writing to CEIC's deputy minister, the executive director of the Immigration Program, J.B. Bissett, stated: "I am concerned both about the lack of an immigration research focus and the deliberate avoidance of policy related work which applies not only to immigration policy, but to all policy."[12] Immigration officials felt that Health and Welfare Canada, especially the Demographic Secretariat established to direct the review, was discouraging any role for or input from other federal departments, including the Immigration Program at CEIC. In an effort to get effective access to the demographic secretariat and to get answers to a mounting number of questions, J.B. Bissett wrote to Dr. Murphy at Health and Welfare Canada. The memo asked when an expected interdepartmental committee would be formed, how immigration personnel at CEIC should expect to be integrated into the demographic review process, and how ongoing contact between the two departments could be formalized.[13]

The uneasiness within senior immigration circles at NHQ was not alleviated by a memo to cabinet that constituted the first report prepared by Health and Welfare Canada. In May of 1986 the unit overseeing the demographic review had been instructed by cabinet to make its first report by the close of that year. This report was to summarize initial findings, identify key research issues to be addressed over the subsequent two years, and outline the research and consultation strategy to be followed. CEIC's deputy minister, Gaétan Lussier, was informed by one of his senior immigration officials that the report to cabinet "satisfied none of these requirements."[14] The official continued: "There is no presentational framework within which initial research results may be grouped under general themes leading to identification of key issues as a basis for soliciting future research proposals. There is no outline of a strategy for research and consultation either."[15]

The sense of most of the immigration officials interested that the demographic review was esoteric and ethereal persisted for its duration. Immigration personnel at NHQ would have preferred an ongoing dialogue with the demographic review participants that gave them opportunities for intervention over the remaining two years.

By no means did the immigration program at CEIC suspend its own demographic work during the time the review led by Health and Welfare was proceeding. Throughout the period immigration officials attended international governmental and nongovernmental conferences to which experts in demography were invited, commissioned Canadian academics to prepare papers on demographic topics, and stepped up internal research on associated topics within policy analysis units of the commission.

As a further CEIC initiative, an advisory committee composed of academics with a comprehensive knowledge of demography as it related to immigration issues was established in 1987. The small group of academics with research interests in immigration matters had, in fact, been part of the annual consultation process on immigrant intake levels since 1984. The academic advisory committee was expected to offer advice on such issues as the potential impact of the demographic review when completed and internal migration and emigration, in addition to the setting of annual levels. The committee was also seen as a forum for the dissemination of research findings. Even though a full-fledged demographic review was taking place over at Health and Welfare Canada, the Immigration Program at CEIC had no intention of losing its own capacity to make informed judgments and to contribute constructively to policy if cabinet asked in the future.

Despite efforts by senior immigration officials to acquire a meaningful participatory role in the demographic review process at Health and Welfare, what contact there was seems to have been marked by a good deal of reticence on the part of Health and Welfare's Demographic Secretariat, and proved to be minimal and perfunctory at best. To balance this assessment, officials interested in demography at Immigration NHQ showed some signs of jealousy, despite their words to the contrary, that Health and Welfare had actually been assigned the lead responsibility for the review. While the Demographic Secretariat had established an interdepartmental advisory committee to coordinate and liaise among departments with an interest in population issues, it seems to have met only infrequently and accomplished little. Dr. Murphy had hoped that the membership of this committee would be composed of senior officials but, as often happens within any large bureaucracy, the chore of attending the sessions was delegated down the hierarchical ladder until only junior officials would appear, if anyone appeared at all.[16]

A certain pettiness or status seeking on both sides can also be detected in the limited, somewhat strained written correspondence between the interested units in the two departments. To illustrate, in early 1988 Dr. Murphy at Health and Welfare sent J.B. Bissett, an official of equivalent rank, a memo inviting him to meet and discuss how the annual immigration consultation process CEIC had then used for almost ten years functioned. As Bissett was unable to attend the proposed meeting, he recommended that another official, somewhat lower in rank but with years of experience organizing the annual consultations, go on his behalf. This suggestion was not especially welcomed by Dr. Murphy, given the already too apparent tendency to delegate the task of attending meetings to junior associates.[17] This was not an isolated example of interdepartmental petulance, but is symptomatic of the bureaucratic rivalry and competitiveness demonstrated by segments of some federal departments, a topic discussed later in this study.

During the first half of 1990 Health and Welfare Canada released the finished product of its three-year demographic review, a document entitled *Charting Canada's Future: A Report of the Demographic Review*. The studies commissioned during the review process were not published in the report but were available separately. The report was written for a general readership and sought to promote public awareness of the relevance of demographic factors to Canada in the final decade of the century. Somewhat surprisingly, *Charting Canada's Future* failed to spark much interest among members of Parliament or the public. The report itself made only marginal reference to immigration policy and contained no recommendations on this subject. The concerns immigration officials had expressed appear to have been well founded.

Internationally, Canada has participated in multilateral deliberations on migratory and demographic patterns. Under the umbrella of the Organization for Economic Co-operation and Development, a committee of experts has met at least annually since the mid-1980s to examine such growing phenomena as return migration and undocumented migrants. Canadian immigration officials have come to believe that international migration and its demographic implications constitute an appropriate subject for intergovernmental treatment.[18] At the very least, sharing information on migratory patterns and other trends associated with developing national population policies appears desirable. Any proposed Canadian demographic or migratory policies must be cognizant of global realities as well as the activities and programs of other governments and international agencies.

During the latter half of the 1980s the Canadian government expended considerably more effort than ever before on the issue of a demographic policy for Canada. At the time, it appeared as if officials and politicians alike had come to recognize the desirability of formulating and adopting a comprehensive population policy. The decision by Cabinet to authorize Health and Welfare to prepare a report on demographic issues lends some credence to this view. Yet no further large scale initiatives in this field occurred. The provinces, with the exception of Quebec, had rebuffed Ottawa's tentative overtures in the late 1970s and early 1980s to cooperate in the drafting of complementary demographic policies. There was no indication that this position had markedly altered as the decade concluded. Ottawa, for its part, possibly taking note of the indifference shown by Parliament and the public when *Charting Canada's Future* was released by Health and Welfare Canada, virtually dropped the subject. Demographic issues had failed to impress Canada's political leadership as being crucial enough to require any further major attention.

PART THREE

The Impact of Structure and Bureaucracy on Policy Making and Implementation

The foregoing chapters have briefly outlined the causes of international migration and analysed the objectives and content of Canada's immigration policy during the years the 1976 *Immigration Act* has been in force. This discussion has sought to identify the goals of immigration programs as well as the many considerations that frequently complicate their implementation. Except for the chapter analysing the refugee status determination machinery, this study has not as yet provided any detailed picture of the structures, mechanisms, and processes through which immigration policy is actually implemented and programs managed. It is one thing to identify and explain the underlying philosophy and particulars of a policy, but quite another to know and appreciate how policy and programs are put into practice. The following two chapters examine the structures, apparatus, and processes that link policy making, implementation, and day-to-day administration, with a view to ascertaining what factors facilitate or impede the attainment of immigration policy goals.

The analysis focuses on numerous institutional and managerial characteristics relevant to Canada's immigration programs, some of which have become contentious. These include the impact of structures on policy making and program delivery, quality of service, efficiency of program delivery, the determination of policy objectives, and impediments to attaining objectives. The next two chapters describe, analyse, and to some extent evaluate the formal or institutionalized structures, intra- and interdepartmental relationships, field-headquarters interactions, ministerial-bureaucratic ties, and organizational behaviour that together shape the processes of policy formulation and program execution. Describing and evaluating policy content must be complemented by an analysis of how the machinery responsible for formulating and implementing that policy functions in practice. Discussing such phenomena requires the selective application of concepts and categories drawn from management science and public administration literature. To some readers, it may appear that immigration structures and mechanisms are assumed to exist in watertight compartments. This, of course, is not the case: many of the issues and factors discussed separately below overlap in practice. The compartments are merely a device chosen for analytical convenience.

This final segment of the study has as its foundation two broad hypotheses. First, the processes by which immigration policy is formulated, implemented, and managed arise largely as a result of the particular prevailing structural apparatus and bureaucratic politics, the nature of the organizational hierarchy, and the values and attitudes held by officials (quite apart from those possessed by the responsible minister and cabinet). Second, within the immigration bureaucracy an almost constant struggle goes on between one group of officials, identified here as "facilitators," and another, labelled "gatekeepers." The degree of influence exercised by either contingent on policy and its management varies over time.

Not only managing the flow of newcomers but being seen to do so effectively remains a fundamental aspiration – almost an obsession – of immigration officials, whether at headquarters or in the field. Every effort must be made to prevent the perception from spreading within CEIC, let alone beyond, that immigrant arrivals are anything but ably controlled and supervised. Officials responsible for the conduct of Canada's immigration programs know very well that the public does not want to read or hear anything about their work that might suggest that major problems exist. As much as possible, the administration of immigration schemes should avoid capturing headlines. For many Canadians, publicity would indicate that something has gone wrong, and could lead to political problems for the minister and the government. However, as profound as the desire for control and orderliness is among officials, the fact persists that Canada is one of the few remaining traditional states of immigration. Both Liberal and Conservative governments have acknowledged that this country needs, and benefits from, the arrival of newcomers who are qualified to enter under the prevailing regulations. Thus, management must also make efforts to put a human face on what would otherwise be an impersonal, solely control-oriented application process. Removing administrative impediments, sensitizing front-line officials to the concerns of applicants and sponsors, and developing user-friendly approaches to would-be immigrants are high priorities for planners and policy makers. Achieving a structure and processes that maintain the necessary control factor while also improving the quality of service for the consumers of the programs are the elusive ideals for which officials and their ministers strive.

10 The Structure of the Immigration Program

Policy making and implementation require an identifiable, tangible structure. This chapter describes the basic institutional framework or apparatus in which immigration policy is formulated and programs managed, with a view to determining how appropriate it is to the tasks required of it.

The shape of any organization, be it a university, a retail enterprise, or a government department, can be most instructive for any observer. The organization's form can indicate to some extent whether the administrative style encourages open or closed processes, promotes consensus on policy goals or contributes to conflict, and reduces or exacerbates uncertainty among policy formulators and managers. Moreover, the institution's design can play a part in determining the ease or difficulty officials and interested outsiders may have in communicating effectively with the units of the system. Finally, the structure can influence the amount of autonomy, sometimes described as "policy space," enjoyed by policy makers and implementers, within the organization and with respect to other government bodies.[1] Thus, this chapter contends that the form of Canada's immigration apparatus has a substantial bearing on the manner in which policy is shaped and administered.

THE CANADA EMPLOYMENT AND IMMIGRATION COMMISSION

The principal structure directing immigration policy formulation and its administration from the late 1970s through the early 1990s was the Canada Employment and Immigration Commission (CEIC), one of the larger organizations in the federal government bureaucracy. The functions carried out by the commission in many respects paralleled those of other federal departments and agencies. Yet, senior officials constantly contemplated how this edifice could be modified to meet immigration policy and program objectives more efficiently and fairly without sacrificing any control or jurisdiction.

Immigration is just one of several policy areas for which CEIC has had responsibility during the era being reviewed here. Other policy areas of CEIC that competed with immigration for the minister's and deputy minister's attention at one time or another have included unemployment insurance, job creation, employment equity and various labour market factors. For the 1990 fiscal year, the approved estimates for the Immigration Program (the formal name of the part of the commission responsible for immigration), including both field and headquarters operations, stood at $480 million, with an approved personnel complement of 4,900 person years.[2] Constitutional deliberations since 1990, altering certain aspects of the division of powers between Ottawa and the provinces, especially Quebec, in such fields as job training, have diminished the commission's size and influence.

CEIC, formerly Employment and Immigration, was established in 1977 and has a top layer unique among federal government departments. To elaborate, the legislation creating this entity called for the commission to be directed by a four-person team composed of two representatives appointed by the government from Canada's employers and workers respectively, a deputy minister who holds the title of chair of CEIC, and another senior public servant who serves as vice-chair. The origins of this type of government body go back a half century or more to the creation of the Unemployment Insurance Commission. As both employers and workers contributed to the unemployment insurance fund, the government of the day gave each group a representative on the first commission, and the practice still survives. Political leadership rests with the minister, one of the more influential members of the federal cabinet. The commissioners spend the overwhelming amount of their time on CEIC concerns other than immigration. Estimates suggest that during the 1980s immigration affairs constituted less than 10 per cent of the commissioners' workload, and even then this time was devoted exclusively to approving changes in regulations. Proposed amendments to immigration legislation or policy are more likely to be channelled through the deputy minister to the minister's office, from where they would be forwarded to a cabinet committee.[3] The bill creating CEIC gave the minister the ability to delegate approval of regulations to the commissioners.

Beneath the commissioners is the Executive Committee of CEIC, composed of approximately fifteen individuals, including the ten regional directors whose territories coincide with the ten provinces. This body operates primarily as an information sharing component of the commission's structure, seldom if ever developing policy or initiating proposals. Like the three commissioners, members of the Executive Committee spend comparatively little time on immigration matters.

Within CEIC, there are commission-wide central service units and branches intended to provide the Immigration Program with necessary support in areas such as internal finance, personnel assistance (including staff development programs), and general headquarters housekeeping tasks. For example, before the restructuring of the Immigration Program late in 1989, immigration personnel used the commission's Strategic Program and Planning Branch (SPP) from time to time for statistical projections, computer simulations, and planning assistance. These and similar tasks are now handled within the Immigration Program itself, while SPP serves the other CEIC operations, particularly labour market research and planning.

For most of the years the present *Immigration Act* has been in force, the Immigration Program's executive director has in practice been the chief official, steering the complex workings of Canada's immigration programs. Prior to the 1989 restructuring at NHQ that created a second office with the same rank, the single executive director, who was equivalent to an assistant deputy minister, devoted all of his time to managing operations and administering policy. Through the 1980s this single executive director was responsible to the deputy minister and guided virtually every aspect of immigration policy formulation and planning, promoted efforts to improve the quality of service, and liaised with the director of immigration and consular services, his counterpart at the Department of External Affairs.

Within CEIC, there are ten regional divisions corresponding to Canada's ten provinces, each headed by a senior or middle-ranking official, depending on its size and responsibilities. These regional heads oversee all CEIC activities in the provinces and, among other things, have the formal responsibility for supervising the directors of immigration, who are answerable to them for the implementation of immigration policy in their regions. The disadvantage of not having the regional directors of immigration report to NHQ is lessened by the substantial amount of informal communication that takes place between senior immigration officials at headquarters and the directors of immigration in the regions. Over the years immigration NHQ has experienced a certain ambivalence about the degree of decentralization desirable for program implementation. This results from tension between the desire to have regional offices operate with substantial discretionary authority when implementing policy and the clearly recognized need to coordinate from the centre so that continuity and consistency are maintained.[4]

Within each region there are district offices, called Canada Immigration Centres, as well as ports of entry at airports, harbours, and border crossing points. It is at such locations that front-line immigration personnel or, in many instances, Revenue Canada personnel acting on behalf of the Immigration Program, meet the millions of people seeking to enter Canada annually as visitors, students, or potential permanent residents. These local operations of the Immigration Program are in fact the testing and proving ground not only for the various immigration schemes and regulations but also for the processes adopted to administer them. It is at the local level, in the "primary immigration line," where the concept of quality of service takes on real meaning.

At CEIC NHQ, talk of structural alteration and administrative reorganization within the Immigration Program is almost constant, in fact part of the daily routine for many middle- and senior-level officials. During the 1980s internal audits, the deputy ministers, and even Canada's auditor-general all persistently urged that forms of organization that were more effective, yet service sensitive be adopted at NHQ, at overseas visa posts, and district Immigration Centres across the country. While there is a persistent feeling that a major restructuring at NHQ is always just about to occur, only two substantial changes actually took place during the 1980s, the first in 1983 and the latter in two stages, beginning in mid-1988 and ending during 1990.

TWO MAJOR SETS OF STRUCTURAL
CHANGES

The restructuring undertaken in 1983 created five branches at NHQ: Operations, Planning and Program Management, Policy and Program Development, Settlement, and Adjudication. This particular reorganization came about partly as a response to the transfer in 1981 of Immigration's Foreign Branch to DEA and partly because of the desire to establish a more professional-looking management approach, in keeping with government objectives for all departments and agencies. Each of the five branches was headed by a director-general responsible for a number of specific program and functional areas and accountable to the executive director.[5] The responsibilities assigned to each of the five branches were as follows.

The Operations Branch supervised all aspects of case review within Canada, as well as the granting of landed immigrant status from within Canada for humanitarian, compassionate, and other reasons. The branch also presented the commission's point of view when cases came before the Immigration Appeals Board and prepared instructions and procedures for generally handling immigration affairs within Canada. The Policy and Program Development Branch undertook tasks relating to the improvement of policy through regulatory or legislative changes, monitored overseas posts to ensure annual immigration targets were adhered to, observed overall annual intake in accordance with the annual levels projections, liaised and exchanged information with regional offices and with foreign and provincial governments on a host of immigration matters, and generally attempted to improve the recruitment and selection of immigrants. The Planning and Program Management Branch supervised all aspects of immigration program administration within Canada, directed housekeeping functions, estimated annual financial and personnel needs and sought to avoid problems that could occur in immigration programs as a result of poor management strategies. The Settlement Branch oversaw the implementation of available government services for newly arrived immigrants, determined needs and established priorities to meet them, and monitored from NHQ the overall administration of adjustment programs offered by regional and district offices and voluntary agencies. Adjudication, the smallest of the five branches, administered the process of conducting immigration inquiries and detention reviews, ensured such inquiries were both fair and effective in keeping with the intent of the legislation, developed guidelines for consistent decision making in inquiries, and monitored and tabulated the decisions of adjudicators throughout Canada.[6]

During 1988 a further restructuring took place at NHQ. Officials hoped that with these structural alterations, the Immigration Program could fulfil its purposes and meet its objectives adequately without further substantial modifications. While not as wide-ranging as the 1983 changes, the 1988 ones nevertheless resulted in the number of branches being reduced to four and some tasks being reassigned. The titles of the four branches were Immigration Policy, Planning and Program Management, Refugee Affairs and Settlement, and Adjudication. No one factor accounted for the 1988 modification. The changes instead reflected the continuing sense, mentioned above, that organizational and administrative alterations at NHQ were needed to improve the efficiency of policy formulation, program delivery, and communications within CEIC headquarters as well as with its regional offices and DEA. Before the 1988 reorganization, reports suggested that officials at district centres or overseas posts were frequently uncertain which headquarters branch or directorate to contact when they required policy and program clarification or interpretation. The 1988 restructuring can also be partly attributed to the persistently unmet need, first articulated as a goal with the 1983 reorganization, to make policy management and control more rigorous and professional.

In the 1988 reorganization, the duties and responsibilities of three of the four branches in the Immigration Program were altered. While the Immigration Policy Branch retained the majority of tasks earlier assigned to the former Policy and Program Development Branch, it received a new director-general, an individual previously attached to the Strategic Policy and Planning Branch of CEIC who had no previous direct immigration experience. The Immigration Policy Branch, reflecting this changed leadership, embarked on a direction less oriented to research in esoteric areas and more to providing practical suggestions and information to incorporate into policy revisions. The altered Planning and Program Management Branch absorbed the responsibilities of the former Operations Branch but strove to approach its activities with a progressive management philosophy, aimed largely at addressing the already acknowledged gaps in and impediments to effective field-headquarters communications.[7] The decision to establish a Refugee Affairs and Settlement Branch resulted mainly from circumstances that had emerged since the earlier 1983 restructuring. In the 1983 organizational structure, Refugee Affairs had had the status of a division within the Policy and Program Development Branch with only a director, a comparatively low-ranking official, at its head. With the remarkably high profile that refugee issues had attained since then, both in CEIC and DEA and in the public's consciousness, the division was upgraded to the level of a branch and had settlement services appended to it. The 1988 structural modifications at NHQ, then, represented yet another attempt to achieve the politically vital sense of fairness and rapid service while maintaining the administratively desirable control over policy formulation and program management and implementation.

However, the goals sought after by the Immigration Program, like those of large diffuse organizations generally, continued to be a little beyond its grasp. These included an improved quality of service, more responsiveness from NHQ to the concerns of regional offices, better communication within the program, and a capacity to deal with surprises and diminish uncertainty. In the view of many officials at all levels, as well as immigrant applicants and their sponsors, any improvement in the quality of service resulting from the 1988 changes fell far short of what was desired.

In the view of senior officials, the 1988 restructuring had failed to rectify the critical problems and with administrative effectiveness and program management throughout Canada's immigration system. As a result, in October 1989 Arthur Kroeger, CEIC's deputy minister at the time, announced what might best be described as a second phase in the restructuring that had begun a year before.

In delving into the matter of why senior management decided this was necessary, it becomes clear that the second phase of reorganiza-tion was always a strong possibility. No detailed explanation of why this was so has been forthcoming from the top of the immigration hierarchy. One plausible interpretation posits that, in case the 1988 modifications fell short of achieving their goals, an additional series of changes was being held in reserve to be adopted at the appropriate time. Late 1989 appears to have been that time.

The impetus for both the 1988 and 1989 restructuring originated solely with, and continued to be exclusively driven by, senior officials at NHQ and not at all by the minister or the minister's office. Resort-ing again to speculation, the change in deputy ministers at CEIC during 1988, from Gaétan Lussier to Arthur Kroeger, may have added a certain impetus to the decision to reorganize the administration.

Whether or not these possible explanations for the second stage tell the entire story, the fact remains that a host of overlapping circumstances and issues contributed to the need for the restructur-ing. In many ways the reasons for the 1989 organizational changes were very much the same ones that had brought about the 1983 ones. By 1989, however, foreign and domestic circumstances had gradually placed more pressure on Canada's immigration programs. Migratory pressures and actual population movements outside Canada had become more pronounced, and demanded attention from Canadian authorities.[8] However, the comparatively small and already over-burdened staff at immigration NHQ did not have the capacity to plan comprehensive responses to such international concerns. Fulfilling their routine duties and putting out unwanted and unexpected administrative fires left officials no opportunity to calmly develop creative and innovative plans addressing mounting migratory pres-sures from abroad. The political and administrative imbroglio created by the enormous backlog of refugee claimants, discussed in chapter 7, stands out as the largest headache for officials at that time, but it was certainly not the only impediment to focusing on other urgent matters. As with the refugee determination system earlier, officials believed that structural reorganization might increase the Immigration Program's ability to cope with these new and intensifying pressures.

A number of factors within the immigration apparatus both at NHQ and in the regions also played a distinct role in creating the need for the second reorganization. For some time, as alluded to earlier in this chapter, efforts (not especially effective ones) had been made to decentralize some of the Immigration Program's operations in Canada. Regional and district offices would have exclusive responsibility for dealing with cases, while NHQ would set and interpret policy and regulations. Proposed organizational changes would enable the regions to receive the sort of assistance from NHQ that they had been promised, while permitting more adequate monitoring from the centre. All this was intended to improve the service delivered by officials in the field and reduce the criticisms so long levelled at the Immigration Program by informed segments of the voluntary sector.

In the final analysis, the increased volume of immigrant applicants, the need for greater planning capability within the Immigration Program itself, and the desire to enable NHQ to fulfil its responsibilities more effectively resulted in phase two of the restructuring.

Just what, then, were the structural modifications at NHQ announced in October 1989? The most important change took place at the top of the Immigration Program hierarchy. As of January 1990 a second executive director position was created, with one of executive director responsible for policy and the other for operations. The Executive Director for Policy has responsibility for four administrative branches, while the Executive Director for Operations directs six branches. This represents a doubling in the number of NHQ branches and directors-general. Reporting to the Executive Director for Policy are the Strategic Planning, Policy and Program Development, Refugee Affairs, and Federal-Provincial Relations Branches. Reporting to the Executive Director for Operations are the Case Management, Immigrant and Visitor Programs, Enforcement, Settlement, Immigrant Support Services, and Adjudication Branches. Finally, an enlarged secretariat now acts in some respects as a bridge between the two executive directors, and fulfils a broad range of in-house duties. This restructuring also entailed the rewriting of virtually every job description for middle- and senior-level officials, a task requiring roughly one year.[9]

In fact the two-stage restructuring was only made possible after Treasury Board provided funding for a substantial increase in staff at NHQ. Between 1986 and the close of 1989, the number of personnel at NHQ rose by approximately 40 per cent.[10] While a sizeable portion of the additional "person years" (the unit of measurement used by Treasury Board) went to reducing the enormous backlog of refugee claimants, significant resources were also allocated to other under-staffed areas. The impact of the 1988 and 1989 reorganization on the processes of management will be examined in the next chapter.

THE IMMIGRATION PORTFOLIO

Any analysis of the immigration organization and structure must, of course, take into consideration the political element, an essential aspect. As of mid-1992, eight ministers had held this politically sensitive portfolio.[11] Between 1985 and 1988, the prime minister experimented with appointing junior ministers, referred to as ministers of state, to be solely responsible for immigration. No doubt he intended them to assist the senior minister for employment and immigration in coping with what had become a most difficult portfolio.

While the prime minister did not explain the details of his thinking when appointing the junior ministers, observers were not loath to speculate about possible reasons. First, the employment and immigration assignment has traditionally been regarded as an extremely arduous political and administrative task for any single minister, largely due to the many diverse programs housed at CEIC. Of these, immigration surely constitutes one of the most politically sensitive, potentially dangerous, and stressful. Second, by the mid-1980s problems such as the seemingly insurmountable hurdles faced by Canada's refugee status determination process, together with the government's announced intention to seek moderate and controlled increases in immigration, may have suggested that a minister exclusively responsible for immigration issues would be politically worthwhile. Such a minister, it was pointed out, could at least put out the fires.

When the prime minister in 1988 discontinued the practice of junior immigration ministers, he again gave no explanation. Observers once again took up the challenge to speculate. The first junior minister, Walter McLean, held his post for a little under one year and then was dropped from the cabinet. He may have been seen as too frequently advocating positions of the nongovernmental organizations in their disputes with his officials over how to improve the refugee status determination procedures. The second junior minister,

Gerry Weiner, served in this post for almost two years and was then given responsibility for multiculturalism. Both Mr. McLean and Mr. Weiner may have felt constrained by their never clearly defined relationships with the senior ministers, Flora MacDonald and Benoît Bouchard. Certainly, particularly during the second half of Mr. Weiner's term as junior minister for immigration, Mr. Bouchard routinely fielded questions in Parliament on immigration matters, responded to media inquiries, and generally did not abstain from involvement in the immigration side of CEIC's operations. With the appointment of Barbara McDougall as minister of employment and immigration in early 1988, the short-lived experiment with junior ministers of immigration was terminated.

The flow of information to or from the minister's office is similar to that found in most government departments. Memoranda from the minister relating to immigration are directed to the deputy minister's office and then are normally passed on to the relevant branch through one of the two executive directors of the Immigration Program. While this is the formal procedure, it is routinely bypassed as the staff in the minister's office seek answers to questions and interpretations of policy matters directly from specific directors or their subordinates. Similarly, when the minister convenes meetings with the deputy minister or the executive directors, other officials with particular policy or program specializations are invited to provide necessary expertise on given issues. Since the minister is responsible for so many programs operating within CEIC, only immigration matters that are deemed to be politically sensitive or that may have an effect on other departments are brought to her or his attention.

COMMITTEES AND CONFERENCES

The House of Commons Standing Committee on Labour, Employment and Immigration, which, strictly speaking, is outside the ministerial and bureaucratic institutional apparatus, is also relevant to immigration. This standing committee is typical of others in the Canadian parliamentary system. Put succinctly, it examines the annual budgetary estimates of CEIC and invites the responsible minister and the minister's officials, as well as informed individuals and representatives of voluntary organizations, business, and labour, to appear and present views on immigration policy and practices. It then prepares and tables reports on its findings in the House of Commons.

The Standing Committee on Labour, Employment and Immigration receives comparatively high marks for its work over the years under analysis here. During the first term of the Mulroney government, in particular, the standing committee proved to be both industrious and constructive respecting immigration issues. Under parliamentary rules and procedures, the government is required to respond to parliamentary committee reports containing policy recommendations within 120 days of their tabling. The Mulroney government was sometimes hard pressed to meet this obligation, as the standing committee issued nine reports over a two year-period on an array of immigration subjects including business immigration, refugee status determination, family reunification, and sponsorship and settlement services. Rarely has a parliamentary committee so effectively set aside partisan political sniping, developing thoughtful reports with practical recommendations that clearly demonstrate the members' grasp of the field.

While it would be an exaggeration to assert that this standing committee actually set policy, it did perform in a manner that caused immigration officials, for one of the few times in the committee's history, to take its work seriously. The reports and recommendations that the committee prepared during 1985 and 1986 caused the minister, his political advisers, and career officials to publicly justify prevailing policy and procedures and to produce credible explanations for why committee proposals had proved impractical to implement. Following the change in membership and chair subsequent to the November 1988 federal election, the standing committee became much less effective.

Two additional mechanisms within immigration NHQ warrant examination. The Immigration Management Committee (IMC) and the regular conferences of immigration directors from the ten regions have both had significant if not continuous impact on the nature and delivery of policy and program services during the years the present Act has been in force. The composition and functions of the IMC have varied over time, depending to some extent on the particular structure of NHQ as well as the style and organizational preferences of the executive director (or, since 1990, the two executive directors) of the Immigration Program. These senior officials have had the responsibility for assigning the committee its functions. The frequency of its meetings and the list of officials expected to participate in its deliberations have all been subject to change. During the late 1970s and into the 1980s, for example, IMC routinely met biweekly, dealt with a sizeable formal agenda, and was composed of up to a dozen or more directors-general and directors from throughout the Immigration Program at NHQ. Executive directors have used IMC as a forum for information sharing, evaluating proposals for policy alterations, and generally overseeing the ongoing administration of the immigration activities that make up the responsibilities of the NHQ branches. For example, during the first few years following the Act's promulgation, when Calvin Best was executive director and chair of the IMC, immigration directorates and branches organized IMC sessions focusing on issues that that unit considered especially relevant to its role in managing policy and programs.[12] On other occasions IMC held extended meetings debating possible options for policy and regulations that would be forwarded to the deputy minister and ultimately to the minister. The committee also played a part in the process leading up to the 1983 reorganization of the Immigration Program. For a time during Best's chairmanship, IMC took on many of the characteristics of an executive board, on which members strove for consensus on how to manage Canada's immigration programs more effectively.

In 1985 J.B. Bissett became executive director of the Immigration Program. Over the next year or so a host of changes took place at NHQ, some of which affected the functions of IMC. The committee, which did not immediately become a core part of Bissett's administrative apparatus, came back to life by the spring of 1987. From that time until the creation of the second executive director position in January 1990, IMC was composed of fewer officials and tended to operate even more than in the past as a senior advisory group for the single executive director.[13] With the organizational changes that established a second executive director and five additional branches, the size and purposes of IMC changed once again. The committee was superseded by a more influential body that acted as a type of executive committee within the Immigration Program at NHQ. This more senior group consisted of the associate deputy minister, the two executive directors and other officials, depending on the issues on the agenda for a particular meeting. As of the early 1990s, the IMC consisted of the two executive directors and nine directors-general and tends to be an information sharing mechanism.

Meetings of regional immigration directors with middle- and senior-level officials from NHQ have become an increasingly important feature of the organizational apparatus. Above all, these gatherings – convened twice yearly during most of the 1980s but more frequently since the 1988 and 1990 restructuring – act as an important link between NHQ and the field. As in all large organizations, public or private, with widely scattered units outside of headquarters, considerable efforts are necessary to provide adequate opportunities for communicating in both directions. However, for most of the period examined here these conferences of immigration directors have fallen short of achieving their aim. Regional immigration directors, as the minutes of the conference deliberations indicate, have not felt that NHQ sought their input into policy matters or that the policy initiatives proposed by NHQ were appropriately debated or explained. Yet officials responsible for improving the effectiveness of immigration operations still consider these conferences the most important structural vehicle for enhancing communications between the two parts of the Immigration Program.

Once the second phase of the 1988 restructuring, announced in late 1989, began, strenuous measures were taken to make the meetings much more than just an opportunity for information sharing. Bringing the regions into the policy making apparatus in a meaningful way appears to have been a high priority among senior NHQ officials. Steering groups were struck to examine and propose regulatory or even policy alterations in a number of operational areas. There has been a greater willingness, certainly on the part of NHQ managers, to let the districts and regions deal with the users of the immigration services and to develop at headquarters, among other things, support for the field operations.

This chapter has identified only the more significant components of the Immigration Program within CEIC. As the foregoing pages illustrate, the tasks assigned to the various elements of the policy machinery have changed frequently as a result of reorganizations and the stamp placed on them by senior officials. In addition to the mechanisms discussed in this chapter, senior NHQ personnel have adopted other ad hoc devices from time to time, such as task forces and special project units, in an effort to address both short-term and chronic problems. These have tended to deal with matters of process and have especially been relied upon to resolve contention within or between departments, to zero in on politically embarrassing issues such as refugee status determination in Canada, and to expedite the arrival of sponsored members of the family class. Having identified and analyzed the key features of the immigration policy structure, I will now examine in some detail the management process that has emerged over the years and that has itself presented impediments to effective policy formulation and program delivery.

11 Managing Canada's Immigration Programs

This chapter moves beyond policy content and institutional structure to examine the bureaucratic organization, prevailing attitudes, and some of the approaches that have affected the management of immigration policy and programs. In the process I comment on structural, procedural, and bureaucratic obstacles in the way of effective and fair program delivery. While an awareness of the departmental and interdepartmental structures discussed earlier contributes to an understanding of policy making and administration, more complete comprehension requires some familiarity with the administrative routines, management modes, and organizational behaviour of the units that make up those structures.

A sizeable body of literature relevant to this and the preceding chapter has been produced in such fields as public policy, public administration, organization theory, and behaviour.[1] While the analysis here draws on some of the generally accepted concepts and explanations appearing in this literature, it makes only a few explicit references to this body of scholarly work. In large part this is because the objectives of this book do not include testing and evaluating the several conceptual models developed by academics specializing in public policy and public administration. To do so would require a much expanded or even a separate volume. My objective here is not to prove the validity or superiority of any one model or approach but rather to examine what impact certain administrative procedures and managerial principles have had on immigration policy and program implementation. What references there are to concepts and postulates from the theoretical literature are included primarily to sharpen the focus of the analysis and point out some of the impediments to efficient yet fair policy and program execution during the years examined. The illustrations at the centre of the following analysis are drawn from interdepartmental issues and relations within headquarters and between headquarters and the field.

This chapter adopts at least three premises or assumptions that together cast light on how the organization of and relationships within the immigration bureaucracy can have negative or positive impact on policy formulation and program management. First, career officials, possibly even more than elected legislators, have a major voice in determining the shape of policy. Not only are they responsible for its implementation and management, they can and do behave as entrepreneurs, directly influencing policy options presented to the minister and ultimately to cabinet.[2] The officials, however, are not always unanimous in their philosophical outlook and policy preferences, which necessitates bargaining and negotiations among them prior to the presentation of policy choices.[3] Second, career officials who are primarily responsible for program management still wield substantial power and use this to control, and provide rewards or disincentives for, other officials charged with the responsibility for developing policy options. Third, two contradictory philosophical outlooks have competed for dominance over policy and its management within the immigration bureaucracy. The facilitators and gatekeepers – the two philosophical camps – present divergent ideological preferences, each producing a different view of what is efficient, fair, and in the public interest.

Informed observers of the Canadian immigration scene generally agree that no matter which political party has formed the government, the framing and administration of policy has not resulted in much partisan benefit. Instead, this process has often brought administrative headaches or even the occasional catastrophe. In the past these problems were usually known only to would-be immigrants availing themselves of processing services and to Canadians trying to sponsor relatives. During the 1980s events within and beyond Canada and the administrative responses to them gradually increased public uneasiness about the effectiveness and fairness of this country's immigration management. By the mid-1980s many Canadians who were not usually concerned about immigration matters felt that the management of policy was, in fact, out of control.

This widespread anxiety about the administration of immigration programs arose in large part from extensive media coverage of the mounting international migratory pressures at the gates of First

World states and the extremely serious difficulties then confronting Canada's inland refugee status determination system. The intense and increasing criticism aimed not only at the content of policy but also at its application represented potential political embarrassment or even peril for the government. According to an in-house report prepared during 1986, "If significant measures are not taken to ensure that the flow of people into the country is being managed and that the program is being administered fairly, then the elements exist for immigration policy to become a major grass roots political issue."[4]

The institutional setting of the Immigration Program within CEIC, a multifaceted department with diverse responsibilities, has to some degree contributed to organizational and managerial difficulties. The Immigration Program has been constrained by the centralizing processes all sections of CEIC must adhere to and, as a result, suffers to some extent from the absence of complete policy setting autonomy. Immigration officials spend a substantial amount of time and effort fulfilling the inevitable administrative demands of the central service and monitoring units that are ostensibly there to assist all policy and operational divisions of CEIC. Critics of the government's immigration policy have asserted that the decision to locate the Immigration Program in CEIC rather than in an autonomous department says much about the importance attached to that policy.[5]

Since the 1989 reorganization circumstances have changed somewhat. First, since the abandonment in 1987 of the experiment of giving junior ministers responsibility for immigration affairs, the "real" ministers have chosen to become very concerned with this policy field and have devoted more time to it than many of their predecessors. Certainly, the time spent on immigration matters by Barbara McDougall, the minister during the late 1980s, was disproportionate to the fiscal and human resources committed to it compared with other policy fields within CEIC. Second, since the late 1980s additional funds have been awarded to the Immigration Program to strengthen middle and senior levels of management and to cope with the paralysing refugee claimant backlog. Third, structural modifications have been and continue to be made, particularly at NHQ, which advocates maintain will make the Immigration Program considerably more able to care for its own needs in such areas as strategic planning. Given the nature of the 1988 and 1989 structural alterations, it could be argued that the Immigration Program is capable of becoming a separate department, the unspoken wish of many officials and informed users of immigration services.

While the departmental setting for Canada's immigration policy and programs represents an ongoing controversy, other factors have had a more significant impact on policy management and service delivery. The remainder of this chapter examines such factors as immigration officials' attitudes, the organizational apparatus, and the procedures chosen to implement and manage programs. Given the opening premises in this chapter, which attribute considerable influence to career officials, their values and perceptions merit attention before analysing bureaucratic and managerial issues.

Public servants are no different from other Canadians when it comes to acquiring values and philosophical attitudes. Their beliefs are shaped by the normal socialization processes, including formal and informal education, their peer groups and other opinion leaders, and the media. In addition to this usual socialization, officials are exposed to and absorb organizational values such as loyalty, the need to prevent any erosion in departmental jurisdiction, and a drive for more resources for the organization, both human and financial. Downs contends that this last trait can be found in virtually all bureaucracies. "Each bureau develops an expansionist ideology which typically emphasizes unsolved problems, unperformed services, and other indicators of imperfection, although in an optimistic manner to imply that the bureau is struggling manfully with its problems but needs more funds to cope with them."[6] In Canada there are also other values, identified by Canadian students of public administration, that produce a distinct type of bureaucratic culture reflecting a combination of British and home-grown traditions, circumstances, and experiences. Among these are political neutrality, accountability, efficiency, responsiveness, and integrity.[7] It needs to be emphasized that officials are not value neutral, and frequently differ among themselves and with their political masters when making policy suggestions or determining how programs are to be implemented. During the 1980s the *Canadian Charter of Rights and Freedoms* and its judicial interpretation have placed added emphasis on fairness and equity in bureaucratic behaviour towards consumers of government services.[8]

As senior officials are routinely required to provide policy suggestions or options to elected decision makers, they have ideal opportunities to have their views incorporated into those policies and procedures.[9] Immigration officials may also apply their values to some extent when exercising administrative discretionary powers, as when decisions on awarding points for admission to Canada are to be made.

At the root of this discussion of values and ideology is the question of how officials believe the immigration organization can best fulfil the responsibility mandated to it by Canadian society and the state.

Put another way, what policies and procedures operate best to further the public interest? On this question, officials vary. Again, a fundamental philosophical dichotomy is apparent at all levels within the immigration bureaucracy between gatekeepers and facilitators. Gatekeepers, for their part, see themselves as controllers and rigorous enforcers of regulations that emphasize the exclusion or, at least, the severe restriction of persons wishing to resettle in Canada. Facilitators, on the other hand, see themselves as serving the public interest by removing obstacles to immigrant entry, promoting humanitarian and compassionate considerations, and adopting a rather liberal view of the entire immigration process. Within both groups examples of advocates and zealots, terms coined by Downs to epitomize activists, abound.[10] While no unequivocal data are available, anecdotal evidence suggests that both points of view are present throughout the immigration establishment, but that the gatekeeper approach is the more pronounced one in the field. There, through discretionary powers, this attitude can have an impact on how programs are implemented and consumers of services handled.

The degree of influence wielded by each of these two schools of thought has oscillated over the past quarter-century. Prior to that, Canadian immigration policy was the exclusive preserve of gatekeepers, with the exception of a very few years at the turn of the century when Clifford Sifton was the responsible minister, and the mid-1950s when J.W. Pickersgill held the immigration portfolio.[11] More recently, facilitators achieved dominance in policy management during the mid-1970s and again in the mid-1980s, and were almost deadlocked with the gatekeepers as that decade closed. The philosophical predispositions of particular ministers have no doubt contributed to the degree of success each contingent has enjoyed.

During the period examined in this study, an additional type of official has emerged. Members of this newest group bring a quite different attitude, one that is less normative and more technocratic. Found primarily at Immigration NHQ, they are most often officials who have spent an earlier period in their careers working as members of strategic planning units at CEIC or in other federal departments. This group has only recently begun to acquire influence and does not as yet rival gatekeepers and facilitators as a major ideological competitor.

THE RELATIONSHIP BETWEEN CEIC AND DEA

In addition to philosophical differences, three factors in particular resulted in bureaucratic tension and administrative difficulties. First, the reorganization of the Department of External Affairs in 1981 had a profound impact on immigration program administration. Among other things, the Foreign Branch of the immigration apparatus was absorbed into Canada's foreign service for more than a decade: Between 1981 and 1992, all aspects of overseas program delivery, including the processing of applicants and the issuance of visas, no longer fell within the purview of immigration officials at CEIC. The transfer of the Immigration Program's Foreign Branch to DEA in 1981 had been part of a much larger attempt to place all the government's overseas services under a single departmental umbrella. For example, joining immigration officials at DEA were Canada's trade commissioners, formerly attached to the Department of Industry, Trade and Commerce. This substantial reorganization of the government's foreign operations was another example of the continuous efforts by senior administrators at Ottawa to refine the bureaucratic machinery and resolve what was perceived as structural untidiness. By 1992, whatever support there had been for this consolidation had evaporated, especially within DEA, and the overseas operations of the Immigration Program were returned to CEIC.

Second, the nature of the relationship between immigration NHQ and regional and district field branches frequently impeded the smooth administration of policy and programs. Finally, the organizational routine, philosophical disparities among officials and imperfectly conceived standard operating procedures at NHQ contributed to inconsistencies and inefficiencies that plagued immigration management. It is not possible to determine which of these problem areas presented the greatest impediment to efficient service delivery or the greatest headaches for policy makers and managers. Together, however, they constituted major obstacles to satisfactory policy formulation and program maintenance.

The often strained and at times acrimonious relationship between CEIC and DEA was undeniable during much of the period that overseas immigration and Canada's diplomatic services were consolidated. While the irritants in the relationship were numerous, the single root of the problem was easily identifiable. One department, CEIC, had responsibility for setting and monitoring policy and formulating regulations, while the implementation and administration of those same policy decisions outside Canada rested entirely with DEA. Inevitably this situation resulted in administrative difficulties for both departments. These difficulties were over and above the sort of conflict large interacting organizations are always subject to.[12] Immigration officials at CEIC had the responsibility for designing and monitoring the processing system through which visitors, students, and immigrants entered Canada. Posts abroad, staffed by foreign service officials from DEA, had the responsibility for operating the processing machinery and managing the flow of persons wishing to gain entry to Canada. These duties, divided as they were between the two federal departments for more than a decade, were carried out for much of that time in an air of controversy and tension, leading to contention and inefficiencies in immigration program management. Officials in two separate and distinct hierarchical structures had to formulate and implement immigration policy under two authoritative heads, in the persons of the ministers of employment and immigration and external affairs. This somewhat unorthodox organizational approach meant conflicts could not be easily or quickly resolved. Widely accepted public administration principles hold that a single, authoritative director is desirable to head any bureaucracy, so as to arbitrate between units whose members may have differing organizational loyalties and who possess goals that are at variance with each other's.[13] In the situation under analysis here, the presence of two ministers with at times conflicting or competing interests did, particularly during the early period of this reorganization, contribute to the scope of the problems. Furthermore, the flow of information between the two separate hierarchies was not without its difficulties, which added to the confusion that seemed endemic in immigration affairs during a good part of the 1980s.

In the view of an internal audit team examining this troubled interdepartmental relationship five years after the take-over, "The decision of the government in 1981 to consolidate External Affairs functions, including the immigration function, in the posts abroad was to bring a fundamental change in the character of the organization of the immigration program ... In effect, the decision cut off the overseas arm of the program from its traditional mold and its developed way of doing things. The decision forced an organizational change on a program which employees had only recently begun to understand and adjust to."[14] Efforts were made throughout the 1980s to tailor organizational structures at DEA and at CEIC NHQ so as to streamline applicant processing and undercut the ever-present criticism about slow and insensitive screening voiced by applicants and Canadian sponsors. The report of the 1986 audit explained that some of the difficulties arose because officials handling immigration matters at CEIC and DEA frequently did not understand where their unit fit into the larger scheme of things, or how the procedures they used were supposed to operate to support the entire program.[15]

One situation illustrating the awkward relationship that persisted between these two federal bureaucracies involved the need to meet the annual immigration intake target. As explained elsewhere in this study, immigration officials at NHQ had developed an elaborate consultative mechanism, which depended on advice offered by a broad range of voluntary organizations, provincial governments, and informed individuals, in an effort to establish what they believed to be an attainable yearly target. The unit specifically responsible for recommending the level of immigrant intake understandably took a good deal of pride in its projection and constantly sought to remain credible. The task of actually meeting this annual figure fell for the most part to processing officials at the various External Affairs posts around the world. As early as October of 1981, just six months after it had absorbed the overseas immigration functions, DEA notified immigration NHQ that meeting the projected target figure for that year as well as for 1982 was improbable. In a memorandum to Lloyd Axworthy, his immigration counterpart, the minister of external affairs, Mark MacGuigan, explained that Treasury Board had authorized financial resources for fewer than half the number of "person years" that DEA had deemed necessary to reach the desired immigrant processing capacity. The minister offered two alternative courses of action to his colleague. They could raise the whole issue in cabinet and possibly prompt a heated discussion on immigration, or else scale down the intake target for 1982.[16] Neither suggestion appears to have been followed up and the immigration targets for 1981 and 1982, and indeed for several subsequent years, simply failed to be met.

Immigration officials at CEIC harboured suspicions that DEA was not doing everything in its power to ensure that annual targets were achieved. Had available personnel at DEA's overseas posts been deployed in the manner most suitable to meeting immigration goals? CEIC officials believed that DEA had shown marked reluctance to assign officers exclusively to immigration functions, preferring instead to have them handle other tasks such as processing requests for visitor visas at the missions, and thereby conceivably preventing the attainment of targets.[17] When annual forecasts were not met, or when fears to that effect were expressed, immigration officials at NHQ found little support for their contentions outside CEIC. Treasury Board proved to be no ally. For instance, it suggested that rather than increasing the number of "person years" set aside for the processing of applications from potential immigrants, the productivity of the currently available personnel could be improved. Expanding on this view, one Treasury Board official wrote, "Past experience ... has shown that there is a great inherent elasticity in the immigration processing system: larger than the three percent shortfall for 1982 which has been predicted."[18] There is little if any evidence to suggest that immigration officials at NHQ shared these views on "elasticity." How DEA officials were deployed persisted at immigration NHQ as the most widely held explanation for the inability to achieve annual targets. The issue reflected the conflict in goals between the two departments and demonstrated the inadequacy of the processes then existing to promote consensus building.[19]

As senior immigration officials within CEIC continued to chide DEA for not meeting the annual forecasts, that department offered other explanations for the persistent shortfalls. DEA indicated that at several overseas posts, rather than backlogs of eager applicants, there were inadequate numbers of candidates, thereby preventing CEIC's projected targets from being met. Moreover, DEA asserted that an unexpectedly high number of potential immigrants at certain centres had in fact withdrawn their applications. Even when applicants had been completely processed and approved for admission to Canada, many of them required a considerable number of months to conclude their personal business and actually depart for their newly adopted country.[20]

Despite these and other reasons for annual shortfalls set forth by DEA, immigration officials continued to feel that External Affairs fundamentally was not trying as hard as it might, and that as a result the Immigration Program at CEIC, responsible for intake forecasts, looked bad. While some immigration officials wondered if internal management problems within DEA were contributing to suspected overseas processing inefficiencies, there was no incontrovertible evidence to support this hunch. Officials at CEIC acknowledged that how the available immigration processing personnel at posts abroad were deployed was the responsibility of the chief of each mission, the ambassador. Nevertheless, the sense persisted that DEA was not truly cooperating with efforts to improve the two-way flow of information between departments and to remove other impediments to the success of Canada's immigration programs.

Throughout the early and mid-1980s intermittent efforts, usually initiated by CEIC, were made to establish an apparatus that would ensure enough consultation and cooperation to prevent or at least limit any conflict in goals between the two departments. At times these efforts focused on the need for a committee or committees to cope with functional, operational issues. On other occasions the need for a high-level committee of senior officials from both departments to thrash out questions of policy seemed to take priority. Typical of the suggestions from CEIC was one made in early 1985, which called for the creation of two interdepartmental committees. One body would concentrate its attention on fiscal and human resource issues of interest to many units within both departments. The other committee would monitor and evaluate the effectiveness of immigration programs and procedures.[21] The negotiations that had preceded the absorption of the foreign operations of the Immigration Program in 1981 had recognized that interdepartmental machinery would be necessary, but the formal memorandum of understanding finalizing the new state of affairs between the two departments did not contain any detailed instructions for bringing this about. It was expected that time and experience would determine the sort of ongoing consultations needed. The slowness with which appropriate machinery for consultation was established significantly exacerbated the problems between the two departments.

Some of the organizational problems between the two departments could be traced to perceptions of the status of immigration officials at DEA. Certainly during the first few years after the absorption of the overseas immigration function by that department, visa officials felt their status to be inferior to that of other foreign service officers. Officials in the Bureau of Immigration and Consular Affairs at DEA experienced lower morale, not seeing themselves as being part of the same team as the traditional members of the diplomatic service. While placing too much emphasis on this issue of status would be a mistake, it nevertheless has to be given some weight in the overall scheme of things.

The many proposals for interdepartmental committees ultimately resulted in the formation of several "ad hoc" groups and at least two formal structures, both of which were co-chaired. The Coordinating Committee on Immigration Program Delivery constituted the operational body that met regularly to thrash out issues directly related to the efficient management of immigration services. At the suggestion of DEA in 1986, a second committee was formed, the Interdepartmental Committee on Immigration Policy Coordination. This executive-level body was composed of "senior officials from both departments to review policy matters related to immigration program delivery."[22] The type of question that came before this policy oriented committee related to issues such as the sponsorship of family members by refugees already in Canada, the eligibility of foreigners wishing to study in Canada, if and when to impose visa requirements for nationals of certain countries, and the desirability of reopening the interdepartmental memorandum of understanding for review. These and other joint committees helped substantially to reduce the suspicions and tensions between the two departments.

However, while the mood between the two departments improved markedly by the mid- to late 1980s, the problems did not entirely disappear. This reality was reflected in some of the conclusions emanating from an interdepartmental workshop hosted in the spring of 1987 by immigration NHQ, and focusing on issues relating to the efficient delivery of immigration services. The concerns of the officials attending the workshop mirrored those identified by the special audit referred to earlier in this chapter. Officials expressed uncertainty about which objectives and goals should have the highest priorities. Moreover, they encouraged all federal departments in any way involved with immigration programs to establish mechanisms that promoted better communications, thereby improving service to the public. Participants pointed to what they perceived to be a lack of coherence among governmental actors responsible for designing policy, training front-line officials, and delivering programs.[23] These and other conclusions made it clear that obstacles still remained.

By no means have all the problems associated with the effective management of immigration policy since the early 1980s been the result of interdepartmental squabbling and misunderstanding between CEIC and DEA. Nevertheless, CEIC continued to have little if any role to play in the administration of its own policy at overseas posts. While consolidating most of Canada's foreign activities within DEA may have had a certain symmetrical, organizational appeal, there are only a few illustrations from other countries that can be held up as successful operational models.[24]

The relative influence of the immigration officials within CEIC when contrasted with DEA in the entire Ottawa-centred government bureaucracy tells a story, too. The Immigration Program is only one segment of this large department, accounting for less than 20 per cent of the total personnel complement. Between 1981 and 1992 the immigration component had to cope not only with the other parts of this mammoth commission but also with DEA, one of the more prestigious and influential federal departments. Conceivably, the Immigration Program officials may have felt somewhat beleaguered in these stressful circumstances. Negotiating and bargaining with DEA counterparts required considerable time and effort from immigration officials within CEIC. For immigration managers at NHQ, the need to negotiate with DEA over how to attain policy goals gave rise to a whole range of those bureaucratic rivalries and jurisdictional jealousies discussed in public policy and organizational behaviour literature.

THE RELATIONSHIP BETWEEN IMMIGRATION NHQ AND THE FIELD

As crucial as the frequently turbulent relationship between these two departments was, other administrative and organizational factors within CEIC itself have also contributed to the difficulty of establishing an immigration policy and program that are operationally sound yet sensitive to the needs of users. One of these factors is the relationship between immigration NHQ and its field operations.

Large organizations, both public and private, with far-flung networks of field operations routinely encounter a variety of administrative and managerial difficulties, often because they do not have mechanisms to ensure a satisfactory information flow.[25] As explained in the previous chapter, the "field," in the case of the Immigration Program, consists of dozens of district offices accountable directly to ten regional headquarters, which in turn report to CEIC's NHQ. Immigration personnel at the district level carry the primary responsibility for implementing the many components of Canada's immigration programs. These front-line officials personify Canada's immigration policy for the users of district office services. The many duties of these officials include helping the voluntary sector to provide settlement services to newcomers, renewing or extending student and visitor visas, issuing employment authorizations, and processing the applications of sponsors wishing to bring eligible family or members of the refugee and designated classes to Canada.

In its 1986 report, the internal audit team had alluded to general problems with field-headquarters relations. Partially motivated by this report, the Immigration Management Committee at NHQ struck a subcommittee that same year to assess the issue of effective service delivery. Its mandate also included appraising the relationship between headquarters and offices across Canada. The conclusions of this subcommittee were very much in keeping with what insiders had known, or at least suspected, for some time. The subcommittee discovered that a significant number of officials in the field felt uneasy about NHQ having access to specific cases.[26] Field officials apparently believed NHQ should have nothing to do with direct service to specific cases, leaving that task to the overseas personnel at DEA and the immigration officials at district and regional offices within Canada. The subcommittee also reported widespread inconsistency in inland offices respecting the interpretation of many policy components and related procedures, apparently because officials did not know where to turn at NHQ when the need to interpret and clarify regulations arose. This confusion proved how poor the communication links were between NHQ and the remainder of the immigration establishment beyond Ottawa-Hull.

The functions of NHQ and the field offices are similar to those of other organizations with multiple branches. The usual contact point between users of immigration services and CEIC is assumed to be at district offices called Canada Immigration Centres, at ports of entry along the Canada–United States border, or at airports. Officers at these facilities are expected to satisfy, as much as policy and regulations allow, the requests of people seeking to avail themselves of the services offered under the *Immigration Act*. Headquarters for its part is expected to advise the minister on policy, monitor the implementation of that policy, interpret provisions of that policy, and generally act as a resource for the field. It is in fact the field, on many occasions, that is first to identify potential and actual administrative inconsistencies and obstacles, through its dealings with clientele.

Despite their hands-on experience with consumers of immigration services, district and regional officials have had little opportunity for meaningful input into the policy and regulatory processes. This wish to be heard on matters of policy and procedures has been expressed most frequently and intensely during the period that the present Act has been in force.

One persistent concern of field staff was the lack of any substantial opportunity to make suggestions to the Legislative Review Committee, responsible for recommending modifications to regulations and, occasionally, to policy. Some regions even established legislative advisory committees to provide input should NHQ actually request it. However, at least during the early 1980s and probably for most of the decade, the Legislative Review Committee seldom requested advice from the field. In the view of its members and of other senior managers, effective consultation would require an inordinate amount of time and would slow down even further the already cumbersome process of review and regulatory alteration. This centralized approach to policy questions typified NHQ style at least until the reorganization of the late 1980s.

For field personnel, irritants abounded. Early in the life of the present Act, one regional director of immigration referred to "duplication, trivial orders, and rules given to field staff over and over again that stop initiative and drown out industriousness."[27] Field officials also believed that NHQ regularly added to their tasks without adding to the staff. Field managers routinely complained that from time to time assigned tasks would overwhelm the available personnel because NHQ requests always seemed to come at once rather than being spread out over time. Districts expressed alarm when unplanned situations directly affecting their operations arose, like the arrival of tens of thousands of Indochinese immigrants in 1979 and 1980 or the demand for employment authorizations for thousands of indigent refugee status claimants in the mid-1980s. These and other problems added to their frustration and lowered morale everywhere.

Other factors have contributed to the strained field-NHQ relationship. Seldom do officials get transferred between the regions and NHQ. For the most part, they remain in the region where their immigration careers began. This comparative lack of mobility results in a certain parochialism that impedes any understanding of the problems confronting both the regions and NHQ. Opportunities for staff development during the 1980s were not plentiful, which may also have hurt productivity and job satisfaction.

These and other impediments to effective service delivery and program management did not go unnoticed by NHQ. As early as 1980, officials at both levels acknowledged that there was a profound need to clear up communications problems among and between branches and the rest of the hierarchy. Acknowledging the problems was one thing: moving authoritatively to resolve them was quite another and has proved to be a long, difficult process.

Efforts to address field-NHQ difficulties institutionally resulted in a gradual increase in the number of meetings at Ottawa to which regional immigration directors were invited. On such occasions headquarters managers not only strove to inform field officials of forthcoming policy proposals that were receiving attention at the highest levels but also solicited their views. At these meetings, the regional immigration directors reluctantly conceded that if they were to have any meaningful input into the policy making process, that process would require additional time. If unilateral decisions were made by NHQ, the regions at least wished to receive prior notice. Subjects discussed at these conferences varied; topics appearing frequently on the agendas during the 1980s included matching occupational demand with the number of immigrant arrivals from region to region, extending family class sponsorship, and improving settlement services.

At the regional level, conferences routinely took place at which district managers and their staffs gathered to share views and learn about proposed policy and regulatory changes. In an attempt to improve communications within the immigration hierarchy, senior officials from NHQ frequently attended these regional meetings and participated in workshops and seminars.

While officials at all levels of the immigration apparatus recognized the need to share information, to develop effective systems of communication, and to adopt processes that made personnel throughout the organization feel a part of it, their efforts continually fell short. Time and time again, at conferences arranged by NHQ and by particular regions, pronouncements about improved organizational processes were heard. In most instances the steps taken failed to bring about the improvements promised.

Throughout the period under discussion, NHQ tried to ensure that regions and districts adhered consistently to the intent of policy and regulations by following standardized procedures and interpretative guidelines developed at headquarters. However, it appears that the guidelines intended to clarify matters were often buried in other directives and information packages that NHQ distributed to the field. In one discussion paper, officials asserted that they were regularly deluged with "irrelevant, unnecessary" information.[28]

That the districts and regions quite properly had discretionary powers in a range of matters markedly complicated efforts to standardize operations and keep policy interpretation consistent. The field, for its part, jealously guarded its authority to interpret questions of sponsorship and other issues of eligibility.

Improving the quality of service to the Immigration Program's clientele ranked very high on the priority list of senior NHQ officials. For years informed observers, sponsors of potential immigrants, and independent immigrants themselves had constantly complained that service, whether at overseas DEA posts or at inland immigration centres, was slow, impersonal, and encumbered with innumerable time-consuming forms. The 1986 internal audit plus questions from MPS added to the pressure for better management approaches. By 1987 the problems had become so substantial and were leading to such paralysis that J.B. Bissett, then executive director of the Immigration Program, felt it necessary to prepare an extensive memorandum for Gaétan Lussier, CEIC's deputy minister. He first identified five significant problems: confusion in policies and programs, loss of equity and fairness in program implementation, a poor NHQ-field relationship, a poor public image, and a lack of quality of service. The memo then addressed the matter of inconsistencies and the lack of NHQ control over program management: "Exceptions to the Immigration Act are so numerous that I believe the intent of the law has become obscured. Equity and fairness have been lost, the public no longer believes in what we say, and neither do we, ourselves."[29]

Beginning in 1986 and continuing into the 1990s, more intensive efforts at NHQ have resulted in a vast array of procedural, policy, and structural modifications intended to rectify shortcomings in service delivery and improve effectiveness across the country and abroad.

Except for purposes of analysis, it would be misleading to suggest that operations in the field are rigidly separated from the structure and role of immigration NHQ. Headquarters, after all, has responsibility for formulating policy, monitoring its implementation, and serving as the principal resource for the districts and regions.

Ordinarily it has no role in directly attending to those who wish to use immigration services. Exceptions occur, as in the case of the backlog of refugee status claimants prior to the coming into force of Bill C-55 in 1989. As one senior official explained, if NHQ does not have a role in serving the customer, it had best do a superlative job in assisting those segments of the organization that do, namely, the field.[30] It is this obligation that, in large part, accounts for the ongoing reorganization of NHQ.

The debate over just what NHQ's structure and purposes should be, as the previous chapter indicated, occupied countless person years during the 1980s. Officials have felt the need to justify to both their critics and themselves the seemingly continuous talk preceding the implementation of structural and managerial modifications. While they asserted the importance of improved quality of service for consumers of immigration programs, they had to consider other factors as well. For example, officials and their elected political masters have indicated that effective controls over the movement of immigrants to Canada must be re-established and maintained. The ever increasing pressure from growing numbers of people, both qualified and unqualified, to gain admission to Canada has demanded still better management of the immigration programs.

Endless models for headquarters organization have been suggested by management consultants and other experts well versed in administrative theory. Arriving at a consensus among these experts and senior members of the immigration bureaucracy has proved difficult largely because of the philosophical divergence between gatekeepers and facilitators discussed earlier. The structural and administrative modifications instituted have centred on establishing clearer reporting patterns within the hierarchy, renaming the units within NHQ and redefining their tasks, promoting or laterally transferring officials with strong administrative track records, and striking task forces and working groups to evaluate existing methods of program management and propose adjustments where necessary.

Although this chapter has examined the Immigration Program's more pivotal organizational and bureaucratic problems, it has, by no means covered the full range of difficulties. Other issues include the attitude of front-line officials toward prospective immigrants, the latent anxiety throughout the immigration hierarchy about a resurgence of refugee status claimants, and the persistent pockets of vocal opposition within Canadian society to the direction of immigration programs. These and similar problems are exceedingly difficult to eradicate or even reduce and cannot be overcome simply through organizational and structural overhaul.

Forces beyond Canada's control already have, and will probably continue to have, substantial impact on attempts to achieve the most efficient yet fair administration of immigration programs. The growing volume of actual or would-be migrants, an increasing proportion of whom are eligible for admission to Canada under one or more of the prevailing schemes, will place enormous strains on every segment of the immigration apparatus. This is already evident as unprecedented queues and backlogs develop at busy processing offices in places like Manila, Hong Kong, and New Delhi. Nor will the pressures be confined to these locations. More and more people seeking entry to Canada qualify as a result of being classified as family members, refugees, or members of designated classes. Others applying as members of the independent class easily get the number of points required for admission, or qualify as entrepreneurs or business immigrants.

Adding to the migratory pressures facing Canada's immigration officials at home and abroad is the fact that fewer states see themselves as permanent destinations for migrants. Australia, for example, while still accepting immigrants, is contemplating changes to procedures or regulations that may limit the annual intake of newcomers. The United States admits few independent immigrants, instead granting entry permission primarily to family members. Since the mid-1980s Western European states have been reluctant recipients of tens of thousands of unwanted, so-called undocumented migrants from Third World countries. In response these governments have adopted restrictive regulations aimed at curtailing this illegal flow.[31] Canada, therefore, stands almost alone as a traditional state of immigration. How long this posture can be maintained is open to much conjecture.

The 1988 and 1989 reorganization at immigration NHQ was intended to enable officials there and in the field to cope more adequately with these changed domestic and external realities. Officials I interviewed during 1990 appeared optimistic that the changes already in place, as well as those not yet completed, would reduce, if not entirely remove, the problems discussed in this chapter. However, it should be remembered that similar confidence was expressed by career officials and their ministers in 1978 when the present Act was promulgated, and again in 1983 when the first significant reorganization of the Immigration Program took place. Given these frequent reorganizations, it came as no surprise when in June 1992 new legislation amending the 1976 Act, again to assist officials in their efforts to manage immigration programs, was introduced in the House of Commons. Immigration is a dynamic process that demands continually changing managerial mechanisms and procedures in order to satisfy both would-be newcomers and Canada's public interest. This newest legislation, which was passed in December 1992 and came into force early in 1993, may, as the past decade has demonstrated, be superseded by further statutory changes before this century closes.

Epilogue

As this study emphasizes, changing domestic and global realities have fuelled demands for an immigration policy and managerial procedures more capable of responding to them. Since the late 1970s the federal government has claimed that its changes to policy and its new administrative mechanisms were designed to do just that. Yet, despite tinkering with both policy and program content and restructuring the immigration apparatus, including the troubled refugee status determination machinery, success in achieving immigration policy objectives has eluded authorities. By the early 1990s officials had made all the modifications possible under the prevailing legislation, without keeping pace with changed domestic and global circumstances. While it would be an exaggeration to describe Canada's immigration system as being out of control, it has certainly been quite unable to cope adequately with either changing demands from within the country or mounting migratory pressures from beyond.

In June 1992 the government introduced Bill C-86, amending a number of sections of the prevailing *Immigration Act*, in Parliament. Following a rigorous debate of the bill's provisions, including the calling of witnesses by the Standing Committee on Labour, Employment and Immigration, the legislation received final reading in mid-December 1992 and came into force early in 1993. Several factors, some more telling than others, accounted for the tabling of the proposed legislation. First, the costs of personnel and programs had reached an unprecedented level. In one way or another, eight federal departments had come to play a part in the immigration scheme of things, requiring 6,200 person years and an annual outlay of over $900 million.[1] Second, new large-scale migrations had developed, originating from Eastern Europe, the former Soviet Union, and Third World states. Other governments of the First World had imposed rigid entry requirements for foreigners in an effort to prevent uncontrolled and unwanted migrants from establishing themselves in their territories. Even with such measures in place, more than 700 thousand asylum seekers had entered OECD member countries without appropriate documentation during 1991 alone.[2] Canadian authorities had come to believe that this country's interest necessitated matching or exceeding Western Europe's restrictive moves. Third, Canadian employers demanded that they be permitted to recruit and bring needed labour to Canada more quickly. To remain competitive, employers wanted the processing time for foreign labourers shortened. Not infrequently, the immediate need that had triggered requests by employers for workers with particular skills had actually eased by the time these newcomers received permission to enter Canada. Fourth, provincial and, even more so, municipal education, health, and welfare budgets were unable to meet the strain placed on them by increasing numbers of immigrants, especially refugee status claimants. Fifth, the late 1980s and early 1990s had seen growing numbers of migrants arriving with fraudulent papers or no papers at all. In 1991 more than 5,000 such people had been apprehended when attempting to board aircraft bound for Canada, while another 6,000 were discovered when they tried to pass through ports of entry in Canada.[3] Finally, the number of refugee claimants making use of the status determination system, including the appeals process, was once again causing concern among the authorities. They could not rule out the possibility of another backlog like the one during the 1980s.

Bill C-86 was not intended to alter long-standing Canadian immigration policy objectives. Family reunification, humanitarian approaches to refugees, and acquiring economic benefits for Canada through independent, investor, and entrepreneurial immigration remained goals. What was required were new tools to enable Canada to meet these traditional objectives in changed circumstances. According to the government, "Over the past decade circumstances affecting our immigration program have changed dramatically, and they continue to evolve in ways that were not foreseen when the current *Immigration Act* was proclaimed in 1978. Political and economic conditions around the world are far less stable. There are growing, unpredictable, large-scale movements of people from one country to another, and an increase in the number of people who want to come to Canada."[4]

As was the case when the last *Immigration Act* was proclaimed in 1978 and when the revised refugee status determination legislation was passed in 1988, the government maintained in 1992 that it was providing new, fair, balanced, and effective management techniques without disturbing the traditional foundation of Canada's immigration programs. According to the government, the new legislation was based on two interrelated principles. First, any fair and effective immigration program must allow Canada to make appropriate choices in keeping with its long-standing commitment to the humanitarian concerns of the international community. Second, these choices must also be in the interests of, and genuinely benefit, the people of Canada.[5] In a background paper accompanying the tabling of Bill C-86, the government explained that the proposed legislation would better permit the needs not only of immigrants and refugees but also of Canadian society to be met.

The provisions of Bill C-86 gave the government and its officials the ability to make regulatory changes that affected how applications from would-be immigrants, refugees, and sponsors were processed and administered. First, the Bill enabled immigration officials to place a ceiling on the number of applications they had to accept for processing in any one year. While the 1976 *Immigration Act* had provided for the setting of annual immigration intake levels, it did not give the government the authority to actually place a limit on the number of applications it was prepared to receive during any one year. As it was, any number of individuals in any of the permissible classes could present completed applications to officials. Despite the possible thousands of applicants already in the pipeline for that year, visa personnel had no authority to refuse additional ones.[6] In the view of senior bureaucrats, limiting the number of applications accepted annually would avoid creating unwanted backlogs.

Second, while Bill C-86 maintained the three broad admissible classes that had initially appeared in the 1976 *Immigration Act* (family, refugee and independent classes), the new legislation authorized the government to alter the processing priorities among these classes when such a change was deemed necessary. Family and refugee class applicants were no longer guaranteed the highest priority in processing. To illustrate, if a need for particular types of skilled labourers unexpectedly arose, a critical refugee-producing emergency occurred, or an opportunity to acquire an unusually large number of immigrant investors developed, the legislation allowed authorities to reassign processing priorities among the three admissible classes. In explaining this provision, the government assured Canadians that adequate consultation would take place before any alteration in processing priorities was made.[7]

Third, under the provisions of the new legislation immigrants bound for the labour market would have their entry to Canada expedited if they agreed to reside in a specific region of the country for a given period of time. In the past immigrants had been encouraged to do this, even to the extent of receiving additional points, but no written promise had been required and the undertaking was frequently not honoured. The new legislation made admission conditional on providing a written undertaking.

Fourth, in an effort to curtail the flow into Canada of people with fraudulent documents or no papers at all, Bill C-86 introduced a number of measures intended to tighten controls. For instance, airlines were required to accept more of the responsibility for carrying people with inadequate or no documentation. Use of the visa requirement would increase where data indicated that nationals of particular countries were more prone to depend on fraudulent documents. In an effort to control bogus or multiple welfare claims on provinces and municipalities, people already in Canada awaiting decisions on their applications for refugee status would be subject to fingerprinting and photographing.

Fifth, in an attempt to ensure that claims were processed within six months or less, the new legislation amended the existing procedures of Canada's refugee status determination system. Since 1989 applicants for refugee status had had to pass through two stages, one intended to establish the credibility of the claim, the second to actually determine its validity.[8] As 95 per cent of the claims had passed unchallenged through the first stage since its inception, Bill C-86 eliminated it.[9] In addition, during the actual determination stage, both members of the panel hearing the case had to respond in the affirmative before refugee status could be granted to an individual who had no documentation to substantiate the claim. Finally, if a right to appeal was granted by the Federal Court, the case was to be heard by one rather than three judges in the Trial Division.

The regulatory and statutory changes that were made in 1992 came about largely because the means chosen to attain long-term objectives during the 1980s had been found wanting. The prompt entry of eligible applicants had not been achieved to the satisfaction of any of the interested groups: applicants, sponsors, or officials anxious to streamline the processing system. Efforts to develop and implement a policy that was fair and yet sensitive to the interests of both would-be immigrants and Canadian society had eluded policy makers. The

1992 legislation, which undoubtedly constituted something more than mere tinkering with prevailing procedures, was yet another attempt to achieve the equitable system so frequently referred to as a goal in both in-house memoranda and public pronouncements.

There is every reason to believe that Canada will continue to seek immigrants. The desire to reunite families, assist genuine refugees, and acquire necessary workers, managers, and willing entrepreneurs explains why this country is still committed to sizeable annual admissions schemes. While Bill C-86 appears to permit more flexibility than did previous legislation, there is no guarantee that it can meet the country's requirements any more successfully over time than earlier statutes and regulations have done. As the opening chapter says, people who find their circumstances intolerable have proved to be exceedingly innovative and imaginative over the years in their efforts to gain entry to countries where they believe living conditions are more attractive. Governments practising liberal-democratic principles, under which human rights are guaranteed by the courts, may continue to be kept scrambling in their attempts to limit the inflow of unwanted international migrants.

Appendices

APPENDIX A
Immigrants and Refugees Granted Permanent Residence in Canada, January 1980–August 1990

	1980	1981	1982	1983	1984	1985	1986	1987	1988	1989	1990	Total	Percentage of total arrivals
CONVENTION REFUGEES													
Government sponsored	864	724	1,384	3,272	4,734	5,276	5,428	6,045	6,417	6,445	4,374	44,963	3.187
Privately sponsored	88	86	412	848	966	890	1,150	1,560	2,400	3,765	2,690	14,855	1.053
Bill C-55/Backlog landings	0	0	0	0	0	0	0	0	0	0	53	53	0.003
Total	952	810	1,796	4,120	5,700	6,166	6,578	7,605	8,817	10,210	7,117	59,871	4.243
DESIGNATED CLASSES													
Government sponsored	18,469	9,893	9,693	6,517	6,729	7,733	8,720	8,229	8,165	8,887	6,154	99,189	7.032
Privately sponsored	21,116	4,331	5,480	3,399	3,091	3,050	4,093	6,002	9,971	17,907	11,597	90,037	6.383
Bill C-55/Backlog landings	0	0	0	0	0	0	0	0	0	0	680	680	0.048
Total	39,585	14,224	15,173	9,916	9,820	10,783	12,813	14,231	18,136	26,794	18,431	189,906	13.463
FAMILY AND INDEPENDENT CLASSES													
Family class	51,063	51,054	50,026	48,764	43,867	38,584	42,339	53,854	51,412	60,771	49,844	541,578	38.397
Assisted relatives	13,537	17,594	11,956	5,006	8,196	7,430	5,911	12,341	15,593	21,520	17,950	137,034	9.175
Retirees	1,548	2,063	2,256	2,095	2,347	2,100	1,838	2,671	3,178	3,565	2,604	26,235	1.860
Other independents	31,556	36,960	33,696	13,185	12,347	13,069	22,748	51,215	49,964	51,574	37,667	353,981	25.096
Total	97,704	107,671	97,934	69,050	66,727	61,183	72,836	120,081	120,147	137,430	108,065	1,058,828	74.528
BUSINESS CLASS													
Entrepreneurs	719	900	1,475	1,865	3,558	4,973	5,881	8,485	11,379	12,984	9,389	61,608	4.367
Self-employed	4,397	5,129	4,889	4,369	2,705	1,522	1,643	2,327	2,725	2,309	1,459	33,474	2.373
Investors	0	0	0	0	0	0	23	319	1,028	2,271	3,137	6,778	0.480
Total	5,116	6,029	6,364	6,234	6,263	6,495	7,547	11,131	15,132	17,564	13,985	101,860	7.220
TOTAL	143,357	128,734	121,267	89,320	88,510	84,627	99,774	153,048	162,232	191,998	147,598	1,410,465	

Source: Compiled from data provided by the Immigration Policy Division, Immigration NHQ, CEIC.

APPENDIX B
Application Processing Times
from Receipt to Final Disposition (days)

Year	No. of Days
1984	220
1985	229
1986	227
1987	201
1988	228
1989	259
1990[a]	303

Source: Compiled from data provided by the Immigration Policy Division, Immigration NHQ, CEIC.
[a] Data for 1990 are complete but not verified.

APPENDIX C
Actual Arrivals (All Categories)
versus Targets

Year	Target	Actual
1980	120,000	143,117
1981	130–140,000	128,618
1982	130–140,000	121,147
1983	105–110,000	89,157
1984	90–95,000	88,239
1985	85–90,000	84,302
1986	105–115,000	99,219
1987	115–125,000	152,098
1988	125–135,000	169,121
1989	150–160,000	192,001
1990	165–175,000	213,611

Source: Data from the Annual Reports to Parliament on Future Immigration Levels, 1980–90 and 1991–95.

APPENDIX D
Immigration Program Organization Chart, 1983

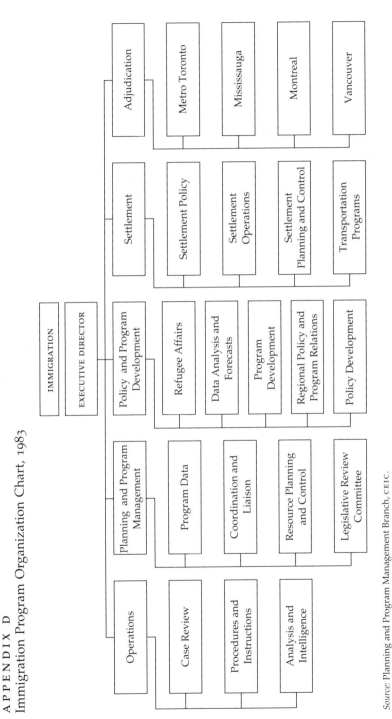

Source: Planning and Program Management Branch, CEIC.

APPENDIX E
Immigration Program Organization Chart, 1990

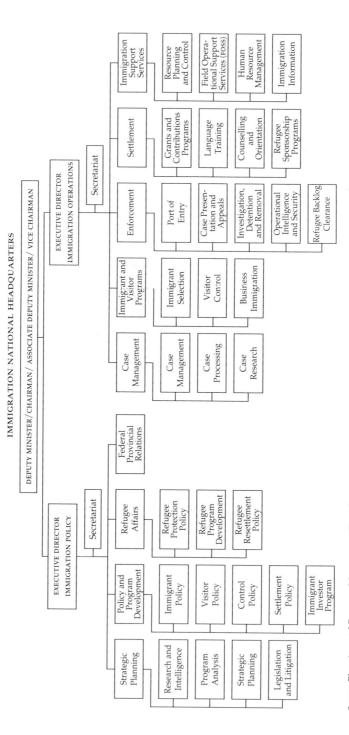

IMMIGRATION NATIONAL HEADQUARTERS

DEPUTY MINISTER/CHAIRMAN/ASSOCIATE DEPUTY MINISTER/VICE CHAIRMAN

EXECUTIVE DIRECTOR
IMMIGRATION POLICY

EXECUTIVE DIRECTOR
IMMIGRATION OPERATIONS

Secretariat

Federal Provincial Relations

Refugee Affairs
- Refugee Protection Policy
- Refugee Program Development
- Refugee Resettlement Policy

Policy and Program Development
- Immigrant Policy
- Visitor Policy
- Control Policy
- Settlement Policy
- Immigrant Investor Program

Strategic Planning
- Research and Intelligence
- Program Analysis
- Strategic Planning
- Legislation and Litigation

Secretariat

Case Management
- Case Management
- Case Processing
- Case Research

Immigrant and Visitor Programs
- Immigrant Selection
- Visitor Control
- Business Immigration

Enforcement
- Port of Entry
- Case Presentation and Appeals
- Investigation, Detention and Removal
- Operational Intelligence and Security
- Refugee Backlog Clearance

Settlement
- Grants and Contributions Programs
- Language Training
- Counselling and Orientation
- Refugee Sponsorship Programs

Immigration Support Services
- Resource Planning and Control
- Field Operational Support Services (FOSS)
- Human Resource Management
- Immigration Information

Source: Planning and Program Management Branch, CEIC.

Ministers of Employment and Immigration,
September 1976 – November 1993

J.S.G. (Bud) Cullen	14 September 1976 – 3 June 1979
Ronald Atkey	4 June 1979 – 2 March 1980
Lloyd Axworthy	3 March 1980 – 11 August 1983
John Roberts	12 August 1983 – 16 September 1984
Flora MacDonald	17 September 1984 – 9 July 1986
Benoît Bouchard	10 July 1986 – 30 March 1988
Barbara McDougall	31 March 1988 – 20 April 1991
Bernard Valcourt	21 April 1991 – 4 November 1993

Ministers of State for Immigration

Walter McLean	August 1985 – June 1986
Gerry Weiner	June 1986 – March 1988

Notes

ABBREVIATIONS

CEIC Canada Employment and Immigration Commission
DEA Department of External Affairs
IMC Immigration Management Committee
NHQ (CEIC's) National Headquarters

CHAPTER ONE

1 For an indication of various approaches used to examine migratory phenomena, see Jackson, *Migration*.
2 McNeill and Adams, *Human Migration*.
3 Hammar, *European Immigration Policy*.

CHAPTER TWO

1 For Canadian population figures since Confederation, see *Canada Yearbook 1988*, chap. 2, 14.
2 Samuel, *Third World Immigration*, 2. For a detailed discussion of immigration to Canada in the first half of the twentieth century, see Corbett, *Canada's Immigration Policy*; England, *Central European Immigrants in Canada*; Dirks, *Canada's Refugee Policy*.
3 House of Commons, *Debates*, 1 May 1947, 2644–47.
4 Hawkins, *Canada and Immigration*, 162–3.
5 Samuel, *Third World Immigration*, 2.

6 Hawkins, *Canada and Immigration.*

7 Green, *Immigration and the Postwar Canadian Economy.*

8 For a discussion of the process of putting a new immigration act together, see Hawkins, *The Critical Years in Immigration*, 42–65.

9 CEIC, *New Directions: A Look at Canada's New Immigration Act and Regulations*, 12–13.

10 CEIC, *Postwar Canadian Attitudes Toward Immigration*, 10.

11 Ibid., 18.

CHAPTER THREE

1 CEIC, *New Directions: A Look at Canada's New Immigration Act and Regulations*, 2–3.

2 Ibid., 12.

3 CEIC, f.8585–1, Internal Memorandum, 16 November 1978.

4 Ibid.

5 For additional information on processing times, see appendix B.

6 CEIC, f.8585–8, Internal Memorandum, 31 January 1984.

7 CEIC, f.8585–8, Memorandum to the Minister, 30 March 1984.

8 CEIC, f.8585–8, Memorandum from the Minister, 16 May 1984.

9 Canada, *Immigration Act*, s. 3(*g*). All references are to R.S.C. 1985, c. I-2. In this revision, the official short title of the *Immigration Act, 1976* became simply *Immigration Act.*

10 Nash, *International Refugee Pressures and Canada's Public Policy Response*, 41.

11 CEIC, *Annual Report to Parliament on Future Immigration Levels, 1991–1995*, 10.

12 For elaboration see Dirks, "The Plight of the Homeless" and "A Policy within a Policy."

13 CEIC, f.8620–1, Internal Memorandum, 28 October 1977.

14 CEIC, f.8620–4, Internal Memorandum, 16 October 1985.

15 CEIC, f.8588–1, Internal Memorandum, 28 May 1987.

16 CEIC, *Annual Report to Parliament on Future Immigration Levels 1990*, 13.

CHAPTER FOUR

1 Canada, *Immigration Act*, s. 7.

2 CEIC, Immigration Plan, *Annual Report to Parliament on Future Immigration Levels, 1991–1995*; interview with immigration officials, NHQ, 9 July 1992. The term "immigration officials" refers to staff of the Immigration Program at CEIC. All interviews with immigration officials cited in this book were conducted at the Program's national head-

quarters in Hull between 1987 and 1992, and on condition that interviewees remain anonymous.

3 *Report of the Auditor-General of Canada to the House of Commons for the year ending 31 March 1990*, 306–7.

4 CEIC, *Immigration Levels Planning: The First Decade*, 8.

5 Interviews with immigration officials, NHQ, 27–28 November 1990; Health and Welfare Canada, *Charting Canada's Future*. This review is discussed in chapter 9.

6 CEIC, f.8000–0, Internal Memorandum, 8 April 1978.

7 CEIC, f.8000–0, Internal Memorandum, 28 June 1979.

8 Interviews with directors and directors-general, NHQ, 8 November 1988. For the structure of CEIC, see chapter 10.

9 For a discussion of DEA's role in immigration, see chapter 11. For a discussion of DEA's 1981 reorganization, see Nossal, *The Politics of Canadian Foreign Policy*, 210–14.

10 CEIC, f.8360–3, Internal Memorandum, 10 November 1981.

11 CEIC, f.8555–5, Report on Processing Time, October 1986; Appendix B.

12 CEIC, f.8360–3, Internal Memorandum, 26 January 1984.

13 Ibid.

14 House of Commons, *Debates*, 27 June 1985, 6268.

15 CEIC, f.8360–3, Internal Memorandum, 5 November 1985.

16 Ibid.

17 *Report of the Auditor-General of Canada to the House of Commons for the year ending 31 March 1990*, 305–7.

18 Interviews with representatives of the Inter-Church Committee on Refugees, Toronto, 8 December 1988.

19 CEIC, *A Consultative Strategy for Immigration Levels Determination*, 1–2.

20 Ibid., 4.

21 CEIC, *Annual Report to Parliament on Future Immigration Levels 1990*, 1.

22 Ibid., 13–14.

23 CEIC, f.8360–3–1, Internal Memorandum, 5 June 1986.

CHAPTER FIVE

1 Nash, *International Refugee Pressures and Canada's Public Policy Response*, 1.

2 CEIC, f.8395–8, Internal Memorandum, 22 November 1976.

3 CEIC, f.8395–8, Internal Memorandum, 9 March 1982.

4 CEIC, f.8395–8, Internal Memorandum, 9 February 1978.

5 Ibid.

6 Ibid.

7 CEIC, f.8395–8, Internal Memorandum, 22 September 1982.

8 CEIC, f.8395–8, Internal Memorandum, 2 April 1987.

9 CEIC, f.8395–8, Internal Memorandum, 25 May 1983.

10 CEIC, f.8395–8, Memorandum to the Minister, 15 February 1984.

11 Interview with representatives of the Inter-Church Committee on Refugees, Toronto, 8 December 1988.

12 CEIC, f.8395–8, Internal Memorandum, 2 March 1987.

13 Ibid.

14 CEIC, f.8395–8, CP Air to the Minister of Employment and Immigration, 9 February 1987.

15 CEIC, f.8255–2, Memorandum to the Minister, 15 February 1977.

16 CEIC, f.8255–2, Applications within Canada: A Discussion Paper, April 1987.

17 CEIC, f.8255–2, Internal Memorandum, 24 January 1979.

18 CEIC, f.8255–2, Internal Memorandum, 17 November 1978.

19 CEIC, f.8255–2, Internal Memorandum, 29 September 1986.

20 CEIC, f.8255–2, Applications within Canada: A Discussion Paper, April 1987.

21 CEIC, f.8255–2, Internal Memorandum, 17 March 1988.

CHAPTER SIX

1 According to the widely accepted definition in the 1951 Convention Relating to the Status of Refugees, a refugee is "anyone who owing to a well founded fear of being persecuted for reasons of race, religion, nationality, membership in a particular social group or political opinion, is outside the country of his nationality and is unable or, owing to such fear, is unwilling to avail himself of the protection of that country."

2 For a comprehensive discussion of these postwar refugee movements to Canada, see Dirks, *Canada's Refugee Policy*, chaps. 7, 9, and 11.

3 CEIC, *Report on the 1991–1995 Immigration Levels Consultations*, 6.

4 CEIC, *Annual Report to Parliament on Future Immigration Levels, 1982*, 6.

5 Interviews with immigration officials, NHQ, 27–28 November 1990.

6 CEIC, f.8620–1, Internal Memorandum, 18 June 1979.

7 CEIC, f.8620–1, Proposed Canadian Refugee Strategy, a Discussion Paper, 14 July 1981.

8 CEIC, f.8620–4, A Strategy for Refugees, June 1981.

9 CEIC, *Refugee Perspectives 1986–1987*, 5.

10 Nash, *International Refugee Pressures and Canada's Public Policy Response*, 40.

11 For a comprehensive discussion of the Canadian programs for the Indo-Chinese designated classes, see Adelman, *Canada and the Indo-Chinese Refugees*, and Dirks, "The Plight of the Homeless."

12 CEIC, f.8585–270, Memorandum to the Minister, 13 January 1977, and Internal Memorandum, 12 August 1977.

13 CEIC, f.8585–270, Internal Memorandum, 9 March 1981.
14 CEIC, f.8585–270, Memorandum to the Minister, 26 March 1982.
15 CEIC, f.8585–270, Internal Memorandum, 10 December 1982.
16 CEIC, *Refugee Perspectives 1984–1985*, 7.
17 CEIC, *Refugee Perspectives 1986–1987*, 33.
18 CEIC, f.8585–7–033, Memorandum from DEA to CEIC, 21 October 1981.
19 CEIC, *Refugee Perspectives 1984–1985*, 13.
20 CEIC, *Refugee Perspectives 1985–1986*, 16.
21 CEIC, f.8005–2, Internal Memorandum, 15 June 1987.
22 CEIC, *Refugee Perspectives 1984–1985*, 14.
23 House of Commons, *Debates* (1981), 12534.
24 CEIC, *Annual Report to Parliament on Future Immigration Levels, 1982*, 37.
25 CEIC, *Refugee Perspectives 1984–1985*, 16.
26 CEIC, f.8570–544, Internal Memorandum, 19 February 1984.
27 CEIC, f.8570–544, Memorandum to the Minister, 10 April 1984.
28 CEIC, f.8570–544, Internal Memorandum, 4 July 1984.
29 CEIC, *Refugee Perspectives 1987–88*, 40, 50.
30 Interviews with immigration officials, NHQ, 27–28 November 1990.

CHAPTER SEVEN

1 CEIC, f.8625–0, Internal Memorandum, 4 May 1977.
2 For a detailed description of the refugee status determination process as set out in the *Immigration Act, 1976* and its regulations, see Dirks, "A Policy within a Policy," 279–307, and Nash, *International Refugee Pressures and Canada's Public Policy Response*, 36–64.
3 CEIC, f.5882–16, Letter from an Immigration official to George Cram, 16 April 1977.
4 CEIC, f.5882–16, Internal Memorandum, 7 June 1977.
5 CEIC, f.8620–1, Internal Memorandum, 14 May 1984.
6 Ibid.
7 CEIC, f.8620–4, Internal Memorandum, 13 January 1984.
8 CEIC, f.8620–4, Memorandum to the Minister, 4 January 1985.
9 Ibid.
10 CEIC, f.8625–0, Internal Memorandum, 15 September 1978.
11 CEIC, f.8625–0, Internal Memorandum, 5 June 1979.
12 CEIC, f.8625–0, Internal Memorandum, 29 November 1979.
13 CEIC, The Refugee Status Determination Process, *A Report of the Task Force on Immigration Practices and Procedures*, 1.
14 Ibid., 5.
15 Ibid., 7.
16 CEIC, f.8300–1, Memorandum to the Minister, 29 November 1983.

17 CEIC, f.8620–4, Internal Memorandum, 6 October 1985.
18 Plaut, *The Refugee Status Determination System.*
19 CEIC, f.8620–4, Internal Memorandum, 5 May 1987.
20 CEIC, *Refugee Claimants: Analysis of Current Flows to Canada*, 19.
21 CEIC, Press Release (Ottawa, 20 February 1987).
22 For additional discussion of the content of Bills C-55 and C-84 and debate associated with them, see Nash, *International Refugee Pressures and Canada's Public Policy Response*, 64–87.
23 CEIC, f.8620–1, Internal Memorandum, 2 February 1988.
24 Members of the Immigration and Refugee Board at the time it was established received annual stipends of over $65,000, plus other benefits.
25 CEIC, f.8620–16, Internal Memorandum, 11 May 1988.
26 CEIC, Operational manual prepared for the members of the IRB, 1988.
27 Malerek, "Canada Setting New Standards," 21.
28 Ibid.

CHAPTER EIGHT

1 For a discussion of the history of provincial interest in immigration, see Hawkins, *Canada and Immigration*, 177–99.
2 CEIC, f.8350–Alberta, Memorandum to the Minister, 8 July 1977.
3 CEIC, f.8350, Proposal for Joint Federal-Provincial Committees on Immigration, 19 December 1977.
4 CEIC, f.8350–1, Internal Memorandum, 30 October 1987.
5 CEIC, *The Immigrant Settlement and Adjustment Program.*
6 CEIC, f.8770–2, Memorandum to the Minister, 16 October 1986.
7 Ibid.
8 Interviews with immigration officials, NHQ, 27–28 November 1990.
9 Interviews with immigration officials, NHQ, 27–28 November 1990.
10 CEIC, *Annual Report to Parliament on Future Immigration Levels, 1991–1995*, 10–13.
11 For a discussion of provincial interest in the business immigrant schemes, see Nash, *The Economic Impact of the Entrepreneur Immigrant Program.*
12 CEIC, f.8588–2, Internal Memorandum, 13 October 1978.
13 CEIC, f.8588–2, Internal Memorandum, 8 May 1979.
14 CEIC, f.8588–2, Internal Memorandum, 12 May 1980.
15 CEIC, f.8585–1, Deputy Minister of CEIC to Deputy Minister of Finance, 28 May 1987.
16 Ibid.
17 See Appendix A for the number of business immigrant arrivals 1980–90.

18 CEIC, f.8585–1, Deputy Premier of British Columbia to Minister of State for Immigration, 8 January 1987.
19 CEIC, f.8350–2, Internal Memorandum, 13 November 1980.
20 CEIC, f.8350–2, Internal Memorandum, 5 November 1985.
21 CEIC, Press release announcing the Canada-Quebec Immigration Agreement, 27 December 1990.
22 Ibid.

CHAPTER NINE

1 Hawkins, *The Critical Years in Immigration*, 63.
2 Hawkins, *Canada and Immigration*, 380–4; Marsden, "Population Issues and the Immigration Debate"; Daly, "Immigration Policy-Making: A Critique."
3 Hawkins, *The Critical Years in Immigration*, 66–7.
4 CEIC, f.8360–1, Internal Memoranda, 20 March 1978 and 21 April 1978, and an interview with a senior official of Health and Welfare Canada, 9 July 1992.
5 CEIC, f.8360–2–2, Memorandum to the Minister, 22 April 1985.
6 CEIC, *Report to Parliament on the Review of Future Directions for Immigration Levels*, 1.
7 Beaujot, *Immigration and the Population of Canada*.
8 Interview with a senior official at Health and Welfare Canada, 9 July 1992.
9 CEIC, *Immigration: A Policy for Growth*.
10 CEIC, f.8360–4, Letter from Minister of Employment and Immigration to Provincial Ministers Responsible for Immigration, 7 February 1985.
11 CEIC, f.8360–4, Letter from Minister of Health and Welfare to Minister of Employment and Immigration, 23 May 1986.
12 CEIC, f.8180–1, Internal Memorandum, 29 September 1986.
13 CEIC, f.8180–1, Memorandum from Executive Director of Immigration Program to Director of Demographic Review, Health and Welfare Canada, 19 September 1986.
14 CEIC, f.8180–1, Internal Memorandum, 12 December 1986.
15 Ibid.
16 Interview with two senior officials at Health and Welfare Canada, 9 July 1992.
17 CEIC, f.8195–1, Memorandum from Executive Director, Immigration, to Director of the Demographic Review, Health and Welfare Canada, 13 January 1988.
18 For elaboration see Dirks, "The Intensification of International Migratory Pressures: Causes, Consequences, and Responses," 65–81.

CHAPTER TEN

1 Allison, *Essence of Decision*, 67–85, and Downs, *Inside Bureaucracy*, 42–8.
2 *Report of the Auditor-General of Canada to the House of Commons for the year ending 31 March 1990*, 300.
3 Interview with immigration official, NHQ, 18 October 1988.
4 Allison, *Essence of Decision*, 85.
5 See Appendices D and E for the 1983 and 1990 organizational charts.
6 CEIC, organizational chart, November 1983, and explanatory narrative. (The narrative is not reproduced here.)
7 Interviews with several immigration officials, NHQ, 22–23 February 1990.
8 Dirks, "The Intensification of International Migratory Pressures," 65–81.
9 Interview with senior immigration official, NHQ, 22 February 1990.
10 Interviews with senior immigration officials, NHQ, 22–23 February 1990.
11 For a list of the ministers responsible for immigration since the present Act came into force, see Appendix F.
12 CEIC, f.8000–9J1, Minutes of IMC, 5 February 1979.
13 Interviews with several middle- and senior-level immigration officials, NHQ, 8 November 1988 and 22–23 February 1990.

CHAPTER ELEVEN

1 A sample of the literature on public policy and administrative behaviour includes Downs, *Inside Bureaucracy*; Allison, *Essence of Decision*; Simon, *Administrative Behavior*; Simeon, "Studying Public Policy"; Doern and Fidd, *Public Policy in Canada*; Schultz, *Federalism, Bureaucracy and Public Policy*; Kernaghan and Siegel, *Public Administration in Canada*.
2 Kernaghan and Siegel, *Public Administration in Canada*, 138.
3 Allison, *Essence of Decision*, 144.
4 CEIC, *Report of a Project to Review Immigration Issues and Organization*, 1.
5 Hawkins, *Canada and Immigration*, 373–400.
6 Downs, *Inside Bureaucracy*, 242.
7 Kernaghan and Siegel, *Public Administration in Canada*, 282.
8 Ibid., 285.
9 Ibid., 292–3.
10 Downs, *Inside Bureaucracy*, 107–10.
11 For elaboration on the traditional dominance of gatekeepers in determining and managing immigration policy, see B. Roberts, *Whence They Came*, I. Abella and H. Troper, *None Is Too Many*, D. Corbett, *Canada's Immigration Policy*, and F. Hawkins, *Canada and Immigration*.
12 Downs, *Inside Bureaucracy*, 115.
13 Ibid., 49–54.

14 CEIC, *Report of a Project to Review Immigration Issues and Organization,* 7.

15 Ibid., 7.

16 CEIC, f.8360–3–1, Memorandum, Minister of External Affairs to Minister of Employment and Immigration, 16 October 1981.

17 CEIC, f.8360–3–1, Internal Memorandum, 10 November 1981.

18 CEIC, f.8360–3–1, Internal Memorandum, 1 December 1982.

19 Interviews with immigration and external affairs officials, 9–10 July 1992, and Downs, *Inside Bureaucracy,* 49–74 and 112–31.

20 CEIC, f.8360–3–1, Internal Memorandum, 26 January 1984.

21 CEIC, f.8000–9–J, Internal Memorandum, 4 January 1985.

22 CEIC, f.8000–10E-2, Internal Memorandum, 27 July 1986.

23 CEIC, f.8000–10E, Internal Memorandum, 26 May 1987.

24 To some extent, the United Kingdom and the United States divide responsibility for immigration affairs between two departments. In the UK, the Home Office sets policy while the Foreign Office supervises the overseas applicant processing services. In the U.S., the Immigration and Naturalization service within the Justice Department sets policy while the overseas operations, again, are supervised by the State Department.

25 Downs, *Inside Bureaucracy,* 112–31.

26 CEIC, *Report of a Project to Review Immigration Issues and Organization,* 5–7.

27 CEIC, f.8000–9J1, Internal Memorandum, 13 October 1978.

28 CEIC, f.8000–10E, Discussion paper prepared for Headquarters Executive Meeting, June 1986.

29 CEIC, f.8000–0, Executive Director Immigration Program to Deputy Minister, 25 March 1987.

30 Interview with a senior immigration official, NHQ, 22 February 1990.

31 For elaboration, see Dirks, "The Intensification of International Migratory Pressures."

EPILOGUE

1 CEIC, *Managing Immigration,* 9.

2 Ibid., 4.

3 Ibid., 8.

4 Ibid., 1.

5 Ibid., 2.

6 Ibid., 13.

7 Ibid., 15–17.

8 For details of this procedure, see chapter 7.

9 CEIC, *Managing Immigration,* 22.

Bibliography

CANADIAN GOVERNMENT FILES
AND DOCUMENTS

Canada. *Immigration Act*, R.S.C. 1985, c. I-2.
– *Report of the Auditor-General of Canada to the House of Commons for the year ending 31 March 1990*. Hull: Minister of Supply and Services 1990.
Canada Employment and Immigration Commission. Immigration Policy Files 1976–89.
– *Annual Report to Parliament on Future Immigration Levels*. 1979–1990. Hull: Minister of Supply and Services 1978–89.
– *Annual Report to Parliament on Future Immigration Levels, 1991–95*. Hull: Minister of Supply and Services 1990.
– *A Consultative Strategy for Immigration Levels Determination*. Hull: Minister of Supply and Services 1986.
– *Corporate Priorities in Immigration Planning*. Hull: Minister of Supply and Services 1985.
– *The Exploitation of Potential Immigrants by Unscrupulous Consultants*. Hull: Minister of Supply and Services 1981.
– *The Immigrant Entrepreneur Program*. Hull: Minister of Supply and Services 1985.
– *The Immigrant Settlement and Adjustment Program: A Report to the Minister*. Hull: Minister of Supply and Services 1984.
– *Immigration: A Policy for Growth*. Hull: Minister of Supply and Services 1985.
– *Immigration Levels Planning: The First Decade*. Hull: Minister of Supply and Services 1988.

- *The Immigration Levels Planning Process.* Hull: Minister of Supply and Services 1984.
- *Managing Immigration: A Framework for the 1990s.* Hull: Minister of Supply and Services 1992.
- *Marriages of Convenience: A Six Month Study.* Hull: Minister of Supply and Services 1984.
- *New Directions: A Look at Canada's New Immigration Act a.id Regulations.* Hull: Minister of Supply and Services 1978.
- *Postwar Canadian Attitudes Toward Immigration.* Hull: Minister of Supply and Services 1987.
- *Refugee Claimants: Analysis of Current Flows to Canada.* Hull: Refugee Determination Task Force, Employment and Immigration Canada 1988.
- *Refugee Perspectives.* 1980–88. Hull: Refugee Affairs Division, Policy and Program Development Branch 1980–88.
- *Report of a Project to Review Immigration Issues and Organization.* Hull: Minister of Supply and Services 1986.
- *Report of the Canadian Immigration and Population Study.* Ottawa: Information Canada 1974.
- *A Report of the Task Force on Immigration Practices and Procedures.* Hull: Minister of Supply and Services 1981.
- *Report on the 1991–1995 Immigration Levels Consultations.* Hull: Minister of Supply and Services 1990.
- *Report to Parliament on the Review of Future Directions for Immigration Levels.* Hull: Minister of Supply and Services 1985.
Health and Welfare Canada. *Charting Canada's Future: A Report of the Demographic Review.* Hull: Minister of Supply and Services 1989.
Statistics Canada. *Canada Yearbook 1988.* Hull: Minister of Supply and Services 1988.

OTHER SOURCES

Abella, I., and H. Troper. *None Is Too Many: Canada and the Jews of Europe, 1933–1948.* Toronto: Lester and Orpen Dennys 1982.
Adelman, H. *Canada and the Indo-Chinese Refugees.* Regina: Weigl Educational Associates 1982.
Allison, G. *Essence of Decision: Explaining the Cuban Missile Crisis.* Boston: Little Brown 1971.
Beaujot, R. *Immigration and the Population of Canada.* Hull: Canada Employment and Immigration Commission 1990.
Corbett, D.C. *Canada's Immigration Policy: A Critique.* Toronto: University of Toronto Press 1957.

Dalon, R. "Immigration and Federal-Provincial Cooperation." In *Immigration: Policy-Making Process and Results*, edited by B. Bonin. Toronto: Institute of Public Administration of Canada 1976.

Daly, B. "Immigration Policy-Making: A Critique." In *Immigration: Policy-Making Process and Results*, edited by B. Bonin. Toronto: Institute of Public Administration of Canada 1976.

Dirks, G. *Canada's Refugee Policy: Indifference or Opportunism?* Montreal and Kingston: McGill-Queen's University Press 1977.

– "The Intensification of International Migratory Pressures: Causes, Consequences, and Responses." *The Academic Council on the United Nations: Reports and Papers* 5 (1993): 65–81.

– "The Plight of the Homeless." *Behind the Headlines* 38 (August 1980).

– "A Policy within a Policy: The Identification and Admission of Refugees to Canada." *Canadian Journal of Political Science/Revue canadienne de science politique* 17 (June 1984): 279–307.

– "World Refugees: The Canadian Response." *Behind the Headlines* 45 (May–June 1988).

Doern, B., and R. Fidd. *Public Policy in Canada*. Toronto: Methuen 1983.

Downs, A. *Inside Bureaucracy*. Boston: Little Brown 1967.

England, R. *Central European Immigrants in Canada*. Toronto: Macmillan 1929.

Foot, D.K. *Population Aging and Immigration Policy in Canada: Implications and Prescriptions*. Hull: Canada Employment and Immigration Commission 1986.

Green, A. *Immigration and the Postwar Canadian Economy*. Toronto: Macmillan 1976.

Hammar, T. *European Immigration Policy: A Comparative Study*. London: Cambridge University Press 1985.

Hawkins, F. *Canada and Immigration: Public Policy and Public Concern*. Montreal and Kingston: McGill-Queen's University Press 1988.

– *The Critical Years in Immigration: Canada and Australia Compared*. Montreal and Kingston: McGill-Queen's University Press 1989.

Jackson, J.A. *Migration*. London: Cambridge University Press 1969.

Jansson, M., and T.J. Samuel. *Canada's Immigration Levels and the Economic and Demographic Environment*. Hull: Canada Employment and Immigration Commission 1987.

Kernaghan, K., and D. Siegel. *Public Administration in Canada*. 2d ed. Toronto: Nelson Canada 1991.

Malerek, V. "Canada Setting New Standards." *Refugee* 77 (July–August 1990): 20–3.

Marsden, L. "Population Issues and the Immigration Debate." *Canadian Ethnic Studies* 7, no. 1 (1975): 21–9.

Matas, D., with I. Simon. *Closing the Doors: The Failure of Refugee Protection.* Toronto: Summerhill Press 1989.

McNeill, W.H., and R.S. Adams. *Human Migration: Patterns and Policies.* Bloomington, Ind.: Indiana University Press 1978.

Nash, A. *The Economic Impact of the Entrepreneur Immigrant Program.* Ottawa: Institute for Research on Public Policy 1987.

– *International Refugee Pressures and Canada's Public Policy Response.* Ottawa: Institute for Research on Public Policy 1989.

Nossal, K.R. *The Politics of Canadian Foreign Policy.* 2d ed. Scarborough, Ont.: Prentice-Hall Canada 1989.

Perez v. Canada (Minister of Employment and Immigration), [1981] 1 F.C. 753 (Fed C.A.).

Plaut, W.G. *Refugee Status Determination in Canada: Proposals for a New System.* Hull: Canada Employment and Immigration Commission 1985.

Robbins v. Canada (Minister of Employment and Immigration), [1984] 1 F.C. 1104 (Fed C.A.).

Roberts, B. *Whence They Came: Deportation from Canada 1900–1935.* Ottawa: University of Ottawa Press 1988.

Samuel, T.J. *Third World Immigration: Multiculturalism and Ethnicity in Canada.* Hull: Canada Employment and Immigration Commission 1988.

Schultz, R. *Federalism, Bureaucracy and Public Policy.* Montreal and Kingston: McGill-Queen's University Press 1980.

Simeon, R. "Studying Public Policy." *Canadian Journal of Political Science/Revue canadienne de science politique* 9, (December 1976): 548–80.

Simon, H. *Administrative Behavior: A Study of the Decision-Making Processes in Administrative Organizations.* New York: Free Press 1977.

Singh v. Canada (Minister of Employment and Immigration) (1985), 17 D.L.R. (4th) 422 (S.C.C.).

Whitaker, R. *Double Standard: The Secret History of Canadian Immigration.* Toronto: Lester and Orpen Dennys 1987.

Index